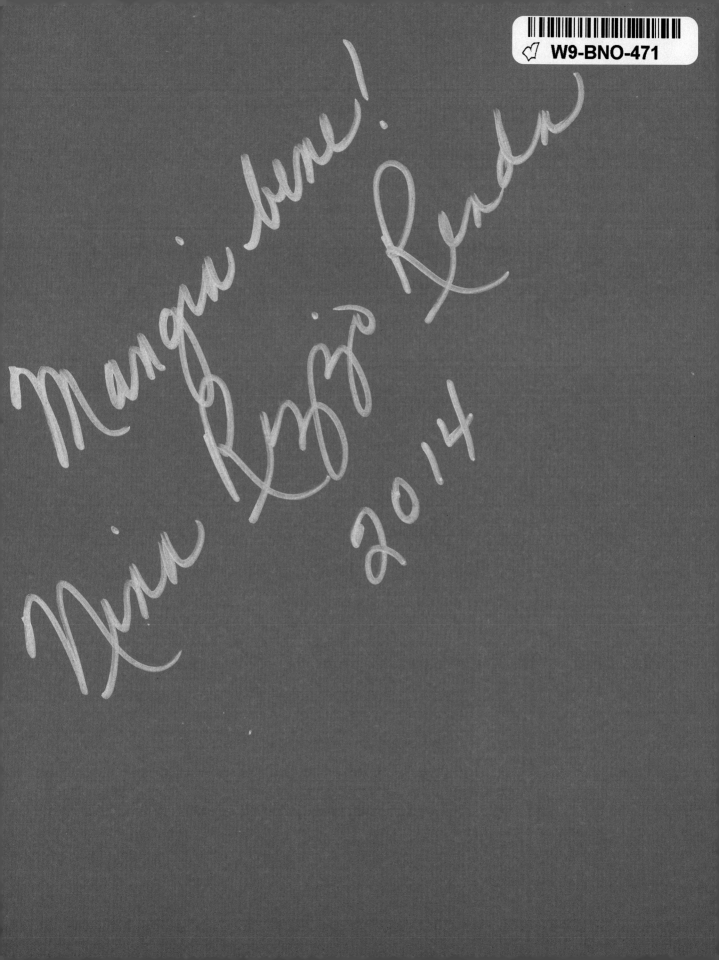

Mangia bene!

Nina Rizzo Renda

2014

Grapevines and Olive Branches

Family Recipes from
The Bernardo Winery

Grapevines and Olive Branches

Family Recipes from The Bernardo Winery

Nina Rizzo Renda &
Leslie May Rodwick

Grassroots Publishing Group, Inc.
www.GrassrootsPublishingGroup.com

GRASSROOTS PUBLISHING GROUP™

9404 Southwick Dr.

Bakersfield, California 93312

www.GrassrootsPublishingGroup.com

10 9 8 7 6 5 4 3 2

First Edition 2014

Printed in China

ISBN: 978-0-9794805-8-4

Library of Congress Control Number: 2013950151

Dedication

*To Mario Renda, who has been our
greatest advocate in writing this book.*

Acknowledgments

No book is a solo venture, and we are grateful to many people for their encouragement and help.

From Nina:

I lovingly thank my parents, Vincent and Elizabeth, who provided the inspiration for this book, and my late brother, Ross, who constantly encouraged me by praising my cooking and making me feel that my food was delicious. I also thank my aunts Jenny and Josie and my cousin Vito for sharing family recipes. We would especially like to thank our editor, Nesta Aharoni, for her professionalism and remarkable attention to detail. She was infinitely kind and patient as she carefully walked us through the process of completing this four-year project.

I am grateful for the support of Ross Jr., Veronica, Selena, and Samantha at the Bernardo Winery, who enthusiastically backed this venture from the start.

I value the warmth and input of my family—Mario, Connie, Tony, and Vince. They have always shown confidence in my ability to present them with delicious meals.

The recipes in this book are from the hands and spirit of my family. I hope our food heritage will please and delight you and your loved ones.

From Leslie:

I wish to acknowledge my mother, Rosemary May, for her enthusiasm for cooking and eating good food. She loved Italian cuisine and joyfully accompanied me to Marcella Hazan's Master Class in Italian Cooking in Venice, Italy, in 1998.

Grapevines and Olive Branches

Contents

THE BERNARDO WINERY 13
THE RIZZO FAMILY 17
RECIPES 21

APPETIZERS

Caponata (Vegetable Relish) 24
Red Pepper Bruschetta 26
Goat Cheese, Fig, and Walnut Bruschetta 28
Green Olives with Orange and Fennel Seed 30
Stuffed Red Peppers 32
Roasted Anaheim Peppers 34
Zucchini con Pancetta (Zucchini Bacon Spread) 36
Arancini (Stuffed Fried Rice Balls) 38
Fried Pumpkin with Mint 42
Carduni Fritti (Fried Cardoons) 44
Stuffed Mushrooms 46

SALADS

Palermo-Style Salad 50
Sicilian Summer Salad 52
Blood Orange and Fennel Salad 54
Plum Tomato and Oregano Salad 56

Dad's Salad Dressing 58

Vince's Salad 60

PASTA

Homemade Pasta 64

Homemade Pasta with Fava Beans 66

Rigatoni with Broccoli 70

Orecchiette with Cauliflower 72

Penne with Escarole and Beans 76

Homemade Pasta or Spaghetti with Cucuzza Longa (Sicilian Squash) 78

Ziti with Eggplant 80

Linguini with Marinara Sauce 82

Baked Ziti 84

Linguini with Garlic and Oil 86

Penne with Vodka Sauce 88

Penne with Pesto Sauce 90

Spaghetti Puttanesca 92

Linguini Finocchio con Sarde (Linguini with Fennel and Sardines) 94

BREAD

My Mother's Braided Rolls 98

Panelli 100

Pane Consado (Fixed Bread) 102

MEAT & POULTRY

Ross's Lamb and Fava Bean Stew 106

Spedini 108

Sausage with Peppers and Onions 110

Chicken Cutlets 112

Sautéed Broccoli Rabe with Sausage 114

Chicken Cacciatore 116

Roasted Leg of Lamb 118

Amogue (Steak Sauce) 120

Braciola 122

Meatballs 124

Sunday Tomato Sauce with Meats 126

FISH & SEAFOOD

Rollatine di Pesce Spada (Grilled Swordfish Rolls) 132

Swordfish Rolls in Tomato Sauce 134

Insalata di Mare (Seafood Salad) 138

Tuna Salad with Oil and Lemon 142

SIDE DISHES

Frittedda (Vegetable Stew) 146

Potato Pancakes 148

Boiled Big Fava Beans 150

Stuffed Artichokes 152

Cousin Vito's Zucchini Patties 154

Frocia (Asparagus Omelet) 156

Frittata (Potato and Red Pepper Omelet) 158

DESSERTS & SWEETS

Baked Figs 162

Giuggiulena (Sesame Seed Cookies) 164

Aunt Josie's Anise Biscotti 166

Ricotta Cheesecake 168

Cubbaita (Almond and Sesame Seed Candy) 170

Persimmon Cookies 172

Aunt Jenny's Fig Cookies 174

INDEX 179

ABOUT THE AUTHORS 185

BERNARDO WINERY 187

Grapevines and Olive Branches

The Bernardo Winery

Long ago, in a valley in North San Diego County, a group of Sicilian partners started one of the most beautiful little wineries in the country. In 1889 Bernardo Winery first opened its doors, making it one of the oldest operating wineries in California. The Winery's heritage stands as a testament to the dedication and loyalty of our family, and as a monument to older and more traditional ways. Now, in our 124th year, we continue to dedicate ourselves to the traditions that have carried us this far.

The Bernardo Winery 1956

Today, the Bernardo Winery is a small boutique wine producer set in a more urban backdrop. We set ourselves apart by making fine wines that are regionally loyal. We use traditional methods that were perfected on this land more than a century ago. Our rich legacy of winemaking started with my grandfather, who passed it down to my father. A century ago, however, wine was produced in an old-world, California style from grapes that were well suited to Southern California terrain. Varietals, such as Muscat and Tokay, were prevalent here and rewarded us with fine, fortified wines that have withstood the test of time. Almost 400 acres of vineyards surrounded the Winery back in the day. Bernardo Winery was once the largest wine producer in Southern California.

The founders of Bernardo Winery saw an opportunity to make fine wine commercially in an area that was replete with richly traditional Sicilian and Portuguese enclaves. Back then, winemaking was as varied as the San Diego landscape, and enthusiasts made wine in their basements and garages. The city of San Diego covered far less area than it does today; a short 25 miles north of the city center was extremely rural. The Bernardo Winery was, truly, off the beaten path. It was part of the city of Escondido and a stop-off point on Highway 395 for people traveling between San Diego and Los Angeles. Bernardo Winery was also the local San Diegan's source for wine, brandy, and fortified wines year round, and for the fresh grapes that so many Sicilians used in the early fall to make homemade wine.

Another large part of our production back then included brandy. Many wineries needed brandy to fortify their products. Because of the cost of shipping, the limited number of grapes, and the small supply of stills, Bernardo Winery flourished as a brandy producer. One large-pot still produced enough brandy to fortify a few thousand gallons of wine each season. Wine was fortified as a way of preserving it, which meant that aging the wine was a simple decision: Make what you need right now, and save the rest. This concept was common among those of us who lived a rural lifestyle. The same idea extended to fruits, jams, preserves, and meats.

Today, the Winery would be nothing without its family heritage. My grandfather bought the Winery from its founding partners in the middle of Prohibition. The Eighteenth Amendment made all winery prices plummet, for obvious reasons. But thanks to my savvy grandfather, the Bernardo Winery survived and even thrived through and after Prohibition. The wine and olive oil production my grandfather started kept the Winery viable and prosperous.

The Bernardo Winery of the past gave birth to the strong traditions we still practice today: *food and wine are life*. We are proud of the fact that our family's dedication to food and wine over the years wasn't just a fad—it was *real* life. We grew vegetables, fruits, and grapes for wine and the table. We used seasonal ingredients. We obeyed the solar clock and the agricultural timeline. Our Winery depended on the land—and on the people to properly utilize it. I never met my grandfather, but when I work on this 124-year-old Winery, I feel as if I work with him every day. The same applies to my father, whom I miss and loved dearly.

My father taught me how the Winery worked: from the antique farm equipment that he once used daily to the redwood wine storage tanks to the rich production mechanics he used to produce thousands of gallons of wine.

My aunt Nina connected the family's history through the kitchen. Our family gathered for dinners on Thursday nights and enjoyed some of the best home-grown cooking ever. Dishes were traditional and focused on what the Winery had to offer in that season. These dinners were beautiful, and I know my aunt enjoys sharing it all with you.

My mother added something to the mix that I continue to respect. She taught me that there may be traditional ways, but that it's okay to pick them up, master them, and execute them in my own style. I have always appreciated that aspect of our family history. I don't expect to make wine the way my father did, but I will always use his techniques and cite his training and experiences. My mother showed me that life is about learning from the best, making things your own, and never losing sight of your heritage.

—Ross Rizzo, Jr.
Third Generation Owner & Winemaker
Bernardo Winery
2014

Grapevines and Olive Branches

The Rizzo Family

I grew up at the Bernardo Winery. It was a wonderful, magical childhood. We were quite isolated there, but our home was always bustling with children, workers, and wonderful extended family and friends. At the heart of my Winery home, though, were my admirable and hard working parents.

My father, Vincent Rizzo, bought the Winery in 1927. He married my mother and moved her there in 1938. Both of them were immigrants from Sicily, Italy, but they each had very different stories.

My father (often called Jimmy) had left a well-to-do family in Sicily to try to build a life for himself in America. He was an interesting and courageous man who embarked on a long journey to a foreign land with hopes of growing and thriving.

After arriving in the United States, my father traveled to Detroit, where he had relatives, and found a job making boxes in a macaroni factory. Later, he went to Texas to join his cousin, Tony Mirabile. "Uncle" Tony and my father were ambitious and decided to try their hand in the nightclub business. It was the era of Prohibition, and they saw some opportunity there. They moved to Tijuana, Mexico, where they purchased and operated nightclubs.

While my father was living in Tijuana, he visited the Bernardo Land Grant on a hunting trip. He fell in love with the land and eventually bought it. Back then, the valley was completely covered in grapevines. Not a house was in sight, and the closest town was Escondido! Through hard work he kept the Winery going until the end of Prohibition by producing sacramental wine and grape juice (which was guaranteed to ferment very quickly!). Eventually, Prohibition ended, and by the late 1940s the Bernardo Winery was producing over 150,000 gallons of wine per year and was a major wine supplier of San Diego County.

My father was a very shrewd businessman, who, although he did not speak perfect English, always managed to get his point across. He was also a devoted family man who had a passion for cooking. On Sundays we held huge family dinners at the Winery. Extended family and friends were always welcome. I remember many Sundays when judges, attorneys, CEOs, and Italian-Americans from all over the country gathered to break bread with us.

My father loved to cook, and he always insisted on having the highest quality and freshest food. He had his beef aged at Talone's in Escondido, bought the best salamis and cheeses at DeFalco's on India Street, and grew everything he could in his garden at the Winery. In many ways, this book is a tribute to him and his passion for the good food he remembered and cherished from his childhood in Sicily.

My mother, Elizabeth Curia Rizzo, was one of seven children. When she was three years old, she immigrated to America from Mazzaro del Vallo, Sicily, with her family. They settled in St. Louis, and she lived there until her early adulthood. She was the most educated of her family and the only sister, out of four, to learn to drive. She worked as a secretary for a large mail order house and came home each evening to a wonderful Italian dinner prepared by my grandmother and aunts.

After marrying my father in 1938, my mother moved to the Winery. Can you imagine the culture shock of relocating from a bustling big city like St. Louis to the rural environment of the Winery? She adapted well, worked hard, and became a remarkable woman.

Cooking was not something my mother enjoyed. My father was the cook in the family. However, she canned almost every fruit and vegetable that grew on the Winery property. Summertime meant canning jars of pears, peaches, peppers, and lots of jam. Each year my father directed his workers to drive a trailer filled with boxes of tomatoes up to the house to be made into tomato sauce. The tomatoes were washed, cored, ground, cooked down, and jarred. The process took many days but produced jars of tomato sauce that we used all winter. Anyone who visited us was treated to Mom's delicious homemade bread and jam—her specialties.

My wonderful mother died at 101 years old. She had lived at the Winery for seventy-two years. She had lost her husband and two sons, but she remained a religious, caring woman with a zest for life.

When my dad passed away in 1971, my brother, Ross Rizzo, inherited the Winery. He had been unofficially managing it for many years by that time. Under his stewardship, the Winery began to evolve into what it is today. He sold 200 acres of Winery property to a developer who created what is now "Lomas Verdes." In addition, Ross also converted all the outbuildings into shops, expanded the tasting room, and began to promote the grounds as an events venue for weddings, parties, and meetings. And, of course, he continued to make wine.

Ross was definitely a hands-on owner-manager. He had grown up at the Winery and had learned to do every job required to keep it going. He could weld metal, fix broken pipelines, repair wagons and trailers, and drive every piece of equipment.

One of the sights I miss most is Ross driving around the property in his golf cart, wearing his big cowboy hat, and chatting with workers and customers. He always had a smile on his face, and he always tipped his hat to the ladies. Ross was bigger than life, an unforgettable character, a gentle giant.

When Ross passed away, he left the Winery to his son, Ross Rizzo, Jr. And so, in the family tradition, Ross, Jr., has become an enthusiastic steward of his father's legacy.

—Nina Rizzo Renda

Grapevines and Olive Branches

Recipes

Sicilian cuisine is simple and unpretentious. It uses ingredients that are in season and at the peak of their flavor. Sicilian cooking aims to preserve the flavor, texture, and wholesomeness of fresh ingredients. This traditional cooking style is so ingrained in Sicilian culture that in Sicily it is virtually impossible to find non-seasonal fruit or vegetables at a grocery store.

Today, Americans are increasingly rediscovering the joys of cooking and eating the old-fashioned way by seeking out the flavors of seasonal, local, and organic food rather than purchasing items that are trucked to supermarkets from long distances.

Ingredients used in traditional Sicilian cuisine include the following: fava beans, fennel, eggplant, tomatoes, cauliflower, broccoli, peas, artichokes, garlic, parsley, basil, bay leaves, oregano, mint, figs, oranges, lemons, almonds, sardines, anchovies, and much more.

To get the best results from our Sicilian recipes, buy fresh, seasonal ingredients whenever possible. Many of the recipes presented in this book can be prepared by using ingredients from your local farmers markets.

BUON APPETITO!

—Leslie May Rodwick

LA PERA MATURA CADE SOLA.

"A ripe fruit will fall by itself."
Everything in its own time.

Appetizers

Caponata (Vegetable Relish)

Red Pepper Bruschetta

Goat Cheese, Fig, and Walnut Bruschetta

Green Olives with Orange and Fennel Seed

Stuffed Red Peppers

Roasted Anaheim Peppers

Zucchini con Pancetta (Zucchini Bacon Spread)

Arancini (Stuffed Fried Rice Balls)

Fried Pumpkin with Mint

Carduni Fritta (Fried Cardoons)

Stuffed Mushrooms

Caponata
(Vegetable Relish)

Caponata is a popular antipasto in Sicily, and everyone has his or her own version of this dish. This is my mother's recipe for Caponata. It was always the "go-to" appetizer when someone came to visit us at the Winery. We served it with my mother's delicious homemade bread. Caponata keeps well in the refrigerator for at least a week.

In a large skillet, over medium heat, heat:
> **⅓ cup olive oil**

Add and sauté covered until limp (about 10 minutes):
> **6 stalks celery, cut into 1-inch pieces**
> **1 large onion, cut into thin slices**
> **1 red bell pepper, cut into 1-inch cubes**

Add to skillet and cook covered (for 10 minutes):
> **2 large eggplants, cut into 1-inch cubes (Peel one of the eggplants and leave the other unpeeled before cutting.)**

Add and cook covered (for 30 minutes):
> **1 small can of tomato paste**
> **1 empty tomato paste can of good wine vinegar (such as Bernardo Winery vinegar)**
> **2 Tablespoons sugar**
> **1 cup green olives, seeded and cut in half**
> **½ cup capers, drained**
> **½ cup pignoli nuts (pine nuts)**

Serve as an appetizer at room temperature with:
> **toasted panini**
> **toasted slices of Italian bread**

Red Pepper
Bruschetta

Grapevines and Olive Branches

This makes a quick, healthy appetizer. Serve with toasted or grilled baguette slices.

Heat the broiler to high.

On a broiler pan, place:
4 red bell peppers

Broil until blackened—but watch carefully.

Remove peppers from oven and place in a brown bag to cool. Once they are cooled, remove them from the bag, peel off the blackened skin, cut off the stems, and remove the seeds.

Chop the peppers, place them in a bowl, and add and mix together:
½ cup parsley or basil, minced
2 cloves garlic, minced
¼ cup olive oil
1 Tablespoon capers

Garnish with:
basil or parsley leaves
4 anchovies
black olives

Serve with:
toasted or grilled baguette slices

Goat Cheese, Fig and Walnut Bruschetta

A crowd pleasing appetizer, sweet and salty with a toasty crunch.

In a bowl, combine and mix well with a large spoon:
4 oz. goat cheese, room temperature
4 dried figs, snipped into tiny pieces (I use scissors for this.)
1 8-oz. jar of fig jam
½ cup walnuts, toasted and chopped

Transfer to a serving bowl and serve with:
toasted baguette, or Italian bread slices

INTERESTING FACT

The History of Bruschetta

Bruschetta's origin is often traced back to Italy, although the exact region and year of its inception is a bit murky. Some reports indicate the ancient Romans used crusty bread to test the quality of freshly pressed olive oil—by spreading oil on a piece of fire-toasted bread. This custom is common in all major olive oil producing regions of Italy, specifically Lazio, Tuscany, and Umbria. Other historical accounts of bruschetta's evolution involve people attempting to revitalize stale bread by soaking it with olive oil.

IL PANE DIVISO É LA SALUTE DEI DENTI.

"Bread that is broken in pieces is healthy for the teeth."
A separate household for the newlywed prevents family quarrels.

Green Olives with
Orange and Fennel Seed

Green olives give this appetizer a salty grape-like flavor and pares well with citrus; can be accompanied by a refreshing glass of white wine.

On a bread board place:

1 cup green olives (with pits)

Pound each olive with the bottom of a glass to crush slightly. Leave the pits in the olives.

In a small bowl, place:

the prepared green olives
1 Tablespoon orange zest, roughly chopped (Take care to peel as little of the white pith as possible when you remove the zest from the orange.)
¼ teaspoon crushed red pepper
½ teaspoon fennel seeds
1 Tablespoon olive oil

Marinate at room temperature (for 1 hour) before serving.

INTERESTING FACT

Olives

Many of the olives trees at the Bernardo Winery were planted at the turn of the century by the five Sicilians who bought the land in 1889. In the 1940s, the Bernardo Winery produced cold-pressed, virgin olive oil from the many trees on the property. Bernardo Olive Oil was used in most of the tuna canneries located in downtown San Diego at that time.

THREE TYPES OF OLIVES GROWN AT THE WINERY ARE MISSION, ESCALANTE, AND MANZANILLA.

Observation:

1. If you pick an olive off a tree and taste it, you will find it very bitter. Olives must be cured before they are eaten.
2. Unripe olives are green. They turn black when they are fully ripe.

Stuffed Red Peppers

This colorful appetizer can be made ahead of time and served at room temperature.

Before you start, check to see that you have some **Prepared Flavored Bread Crumbs** in the freezer (see below).

Cut into quarters, and place on a jelly roll pan:
> **4 red or yellow bell peppers**

In a bowl, mix together:

¼ cup olive oil	**¼ cup grated Parmesan cheese**
¼ cup (or slightly less) capers	**2 Tablespoons parsley, chopped**
¼ cup toasted pignoli nuts (pine nuts)	**2 cloves garlic, minced**
½ cup bread crumbs	**¼ teaspoon red pepper flakes**
½ cup Panko	**salt and pepper to taste**

Fill the cavities of the peppers with the bread crumb mixture, and drizzle with an additional:
> **¼ cup olive oil (or less)**

Bake at 350° (for 45 minutes).

Prepared Flavored Bread Crumbs:

I like to make flavored bread crumbs ahead of time and store them in the freezer for future use. I use them in many recipes. The recipe below makes 2½ to 3 cups of crumbs. *Alternatively*, use 1 cup of prepared crumbs instead of the bread crumbs and Panko, and add only 1 Tablespoon of parsley and 1 clove of garlic to the recipe above.

Combine and mix well:

1 cup bread crumbs (processed bread)	**1 Tablespoon parsley, chopped**
1 cup Panko	**3 cloves garlic, pressed**
½ cup grated Parmesan cheese	**salt and pepper to taste**

Store extra bread crumbs in a plastic bag in the freezer.

Roasted Anaheim Peppers

Anaheim peppers originated from New Mexico; they are considered hot on the Scoville Heat Scale. By removing the pepper's seeds, you retain the pepper's smoky flavor without being subjected to extreme heat. Pairing these peppers with onions and cheese mellows them into a creamy delight.

Wash, cut off stems, and remove seeds from:
> **6 Anaheim peppers**

Cut a slit down one side of each pepper. Divide evenly and stuff the peppers with:
> **1 onion, sliced thinly**
> **8 oz. Swiss cheese (like Jarlsberg), cut into thin slices**

Place the stuffed peppers on a sheet pan and drizzle with:
> **olive oil**
> **salt and pepper**

Bake at 350º (for 30 minutes).

IO SCORZO LE CIPOLLE E A TE TI BRUCIANO GLI OCCHI?

"I'm peeling the onions and *you* complain that *your* eyes are burning?"

Zucchini con Pancetta
(Zucchini Bacon Spread)

When you pair the garden freshness of zucchini and the crispness of bacon or pancetta, you get a delightful start to any meal.

In a large skillet, over medium heat, heat:
> **2 Tablespoons olive oil**

Add and stir to mix:
> **3 good-sized zucchinis, thinly sliced**
> **3-4 cloves garlic, finely minced**
> **½ teaspoon crushed red pepper**
> **1 teaspoon salt**

Stir well, lower heat to low, cover, and let mixture cook slowly until soft (about 25-30 minutes).

While zucchini mixture cooks, fry in a small skillet until crispy:
> **3 slices smoky bacon or pancetta diced into small pieces**

When cooked, remove bacon bits to a paper towel to drain.

When the zucchini mixture is soft, remove from heat, place in a food processor, and process until you have a thick puree with small pieces of zucchini still visible. (Use an immersion blender for this step, if you wish.)

Transfer the mixture to a serving bowl, and garnish with the bacon bits.

Serve with:
> **slices of toasted baguette or Italian bread**

Arancini
(Stuffed Fried Rice Balls)

Arancini—fried rice balls often stuffed with meat, vegetables, or cheese—are a staple of Sicilian cuisine.

Make the Filling:
(or, if you prefer, skip this step and stuff the rice balls with a cube of Fontina cheese):

In a large saucepan over medium heat, heat:
> **2 Tablespoons olive oil**

Add and cook until soft (about 5 minutes):
> **1 onion, finely chopped**

Add and cook until fragrant (about 30 seconds):
> **1 small clove of garlic, finely chopped**

Add to the skillet and cook, stirring until lightly browned (about 10 minutes):
> **½ pound lean ground beef**

Stir in, bring to a simmer, reduce heat to low, and cook until thick, breaking up the tomatoes if they are chunky (about 30 minutes):
> **1 14.5-oz. can chopped canned Italian tomatoes, drained**
> **salt and freshly ground pepper to taste**

Add and cook (an additional 5 minutes), and let cool:
> **½ cup frozen peas**

Make the Rice:
In a large pot, bring to a boil:
> **5 cups chicken broth**
> **½ teaspoon saffron threads, crumbled (optional)**

Stir in and cook until rice is tender and all the liquid is absorbed (about 18 minutes). Stir often to avoid burning:

> **2 cups Arborio rice**
> **2 Tablespoons butter**
> **salt to taste**

Remove rice from the heat and stir in:

> **1 cup freshly grated Parmigiano-Reggiano cheese**

Let cool slightly and then stir in:

> **4 large egg yolks (Keep the egg whites for the next step.)**

Assemble Additional Ingredients:
In a small bowl, beat until foamy:

> **4 large egg whites**

In a shallow dish, place:

> **Flour, for dredging**

In another shallow dish, place:

> **2 cups plain bread crumbs**

On a plate:

> **4 oz. mozzarella cheese, cut into small cubes**

Assemble the Rice Balls:
Dip your hands in cool water to prevent the rice from sticking. Scoop up ½ to ⅓ cup of the rice mixture and place it in the palm of one hand. Poke a shallow hole in the center of the rice. Press 1 Tablespoon of the filling into the hole and top it with a piece of the mozzarella. Cup your hand slightly, molding the rice over the filling to enclose it completely. Add a little more rice if necessary to cover the filling completely. Very gently squeeze the ball together to compact the rice.

Carefully roll the ball in the flour, then the egg whites, and then the bread crumbs, being careful to coat completely.

Place the finished balls on a rack over a baking sheet.

Continue making the rice balls, rinsing your hands between each one. When all the balls have been made, place the rack in the refrigerator (for 30 minutes).

Fry the Rice Balls:
In a heavy saucepan pour in and heat:

      3 inches of vegetable oil (or less)

Fry a few rice balls at a time taking care not to crowd the pan. Cook until golden brown and crisp all over (about 3-4 minutes).

Transfer the balls to paper towels to drain.

Serve hot or cold.

INTERESTING FACT

The Tradtions of Arancini
The literal translation of "arancini" is "orange." Oranges are abundant in Sicily. Arancini were named because of their visual similarity to the fruit.

ARANCINI ARE SOMEWHAT LABOR INTENSIVE; THEREFORE, THEY ARE CONSIDERED TREATS MADE ON SPECIAL OCCASIONS.

1. Arancini can be served cold or hot with additional sauce on the side.
2. They can be made as a walnut-sized appetizer or baseball-sized entree.

Fried Pumpkin
with Mint

My wonderful brother, Ross, grew a large patch of pumpkins each year. My mother created this recipe for fried pumpkin, and the family loves it.

Prepare:
> **1 small pumpkin**

Cut the pumpkin in half. Cut off the stem end and the bottom end. Remove the seeds, and slice the pumpkin into ¼-inch slices. Peel off the skin with a vegetable peeler.

In a frying pan, heat:
> **½ cup olive oil**

Add the pumpkin and fry in batches (being careful not to crowd the pan).

In a bowl, combine:
> **½ cup olive oil**
> **¼ cup vinegar (such as Bernardo Winery vinegar)**
> **½ cup mint leaves, minced**
> **3 cloves garlic, minced finely**

Layer the pumpkin slices in a platter, and drizzle with the mixture. Continue to layer slices and drizzle with the mixture until all the pumpkin is used.

Carduni Fritti
(Fried Cardoons)

Cardoons are the stalks of the artichoke leaves. They look a lot like a big celery stalk. We grow artichokes at the Winery. I have wonderful memories of driving around the Winery in a golf cart (the main source of transportation there) with my brother Ross and stopping to cut the stalks to take home and cook. Traditionally carduni fritti are a part of a Christmas Eve feast, but they also make a great appetizer.

Prepare:
cardoon stalks

Peel off the strings and cut the stalks into 6-inch lengths.

In a large pot on the stove bring to a boil:
water and juice of one lemon

Add the prepared carduni and boil (for 30 minutes or until tender). Drain them. When they are cool, pat them dry.

In a shallow bowl place:
enough flour to coat the stalks

In another shallow bowl, place and whisk with a fork:
1 to 2 eggs (depending on how many carduni you have)

In a third bowl place:
enough dry bread crumbs to coat the stalks and salt and pepper to taste

Coat each stalk with flour, dip each into the egg mixture, and then coat completely with the bread crumbs.

In a skillet over medium heat add:
1 inch of olive oil

Panfry the prepared carduni until a rich golden brown. Drain on paper towels, and serve hot or at room temperature.

Stuffed Mushrooms

The earthiness of mushrooms makes them a wonderful starter. Using two different types of bread crumbs helps to bind the ingredients together while adding a little crunch.

Prepare:
12 mushrooms, 2½- to 3-inches in diameter

Remove the stems from the mushroom caps, and clean both parts with a mushroom brush. Reserve the mushroom caps and chop the stems.

In a bowl add and mix thoroughly:
the chopped mushroom stems
1 Tablespoon parsley, chopped
¼ cup bread crumbs
¼ cup Panko
¼ cup grated Parmesan cheese
1 clove of garlic, mashed
2 Tablespoons olive oil

Stuff the mushroom caps with the mixture and place them in a shallow baking dish greased with some olive oil.

Drizzle over the top:
1 Tablespoon olive oil

Bake at 350° (for 30 minutes).

CHI HA LA SALUTE E RICCO É NON LO SA.

"He who has his health is wealthy and doesn't realize it."
Good health is wealth.

Salads

Palermo-Style Salad

Sicilian Summer Salad

Blood Orange and Fennel Salad

Plum Tomato and Oregano Salad

Dad's Salad Dressing

Vince's Salad

Palermo-Style Salad

Anchovy paste gives this potato salad an Italian twist.

Prepare:
> **1 large onion in its skin**

Place onion on a small baking tray and bake at 350° until it becomes slightly caramelized and soft (about 30-45 minutes).

In a small pot, add:
> **2 medium waxy potatoes (such as Yukon Gold)**
> **enough water to cover**
> **1 teaspoon salt**

Bring the water with contents to a boil and boil gently (for about 15 to 20 minutes, or until the potatoes are fork tender). Then remove to a plate to cool.

When the potatoes are done, use the same pot to cook, and then remove to a plate to cool:
> **salted water**
> **1 to 1½ cups green beans**

To a large salad bowl add and mix together:
> **2 medium tomatoes, chopped into cubes**
> **the cooled potatoes, chopped into cubes**
> **the green beans, chopped slightly**
> **the soft onion, chopped into pieces and mixed with:**
> > **1 Tablespoon anchovy paste**
> > **2 teaspoons white wine vinegar**

Salt and pepper to taste and serve cool. This dish can be served as an antipasti or a side dish.

Sicilian Summer Salad

Grapevines and Olive Branches

Enjoy this timeless salad made with summer fresh tomatoes and green beans. The anchovy fillets and capers give it a briny saltiness without overpowering the freshness of the veggies.

Add to a salad bowl and mix well:

1 pound cherry tomatoes, cut in half
¼ cup capers, drained
¼ cup green olives, cut into pieces
1 small red onion, thinly sliced
½ pound cooked green beans
3 anchovy fillets, chopped fine
6 large leaves basil, cut into very thin strips
2 Tablespoons extra virgin olive oil
3 Tablespoons red wine vinegar (such as Bernardo Winery
vinegar)
fresh ground pepper to taste

Bernardo Winery Vinegar

Blood Orange and Fennel Salad

Grapevines and Olive Branches

When I was a child at the Winery, we grew blood oranges. Each blood orange is unique because the red coloring inside differs in each orange, the flesh ranging from yellow to orange to scarlet red. Everything in this salad grew on the property, so making it was just a matter of picking and preparing.

In a large salad bowl place:

6 blood oranges, peeled and thinly sliced
2 fennel bulbs, thinly sliced
1 red onion, thinly sliced
salt and pepper to taste
¼ cup lemon juice
¼ cup olive oil

Mix all the ingredients together and marinate.

Serve.

PER UN GRANO DI SALE SI PERDE LA MINESTRA.

"For a granule of salt, you can spoil the soup."
The wise person has a sense of proportion.

Plum Tomato and Oregano Salad

A lively yet elegant salad . . . enhanced with fresh oregano leaves.

In a bowl, combine:

8 plum tomatoes (such as Roma tomatoes), sliced into rounds
1 small red onion, sliced thinly
2 cloves garlic, sliced thinly
1 Tablespoon fresh oregano leaves, minced

Pour over the mixture:

¼ cup olive oil
¼ cup red wine vinegar (such as Bernardo Winery vinegar)

Season with:

salt and pepper to taste

CHI PAGA, BALLA.

"He who pays also has the right to dance."
He who pays the fiddler calls the tune.

Dad's Salad Dressing

This robust salad dressing is excellent on any mixed green salad.

Place into a mortar and use a pestle to crush thoroughly:
> **3 cloves garlic**
> **1 teaspoon salt**

Add and mix well:
> **1 Tablespoon Dijon-style mustard**
> **2 Tablespoons ketchup**
> **½ cup vinegar (such as Bernardo Winery vinegar)**
> **1 teaspoon pepper**

Add slowly while mixing vigorously:
> **½ cup good olive oil**

INTERESTING FACT

Amazing Garlic

In Sicilian homes, garlic is a staple. It has been around for centuries, and Italians have used it for everything from deliciously flavoring our cooking to warding off evil spirits.

Garlic is a bulb. In many Sicilian homes, after the garlic harvest, the stems of the bulbs are braided into long strands and hung on a hook.

Leave your garlic out, on the counter. Refrigerated garlic dries out faster.

Vince's Salad

This simple salad is my son Vince's favorite. My father taught me to make this dressing using freshly picked lemons from the Winery.

Use a mortar and pestle to pound into a paste:
4 cloves garlic
1 Tablespoon salt

Add, and mix thoroughly:
¾ cup freshly squeezed lemon juice
½ cup olive oil
freshly ground pepper

Pour the dressing over:
Romaine lettuce, torn into
bite-sized pieces

Sprinkle with:
freshly grated
Parmigiano-Reggiano cheese

My parents, Vince and Elizabeth's Wedding Picture

AMICI E MACCHERONI, SE NON SONO CALDI,
NON SONO BUONI.

"Friends, like macaroni, if they're not warm, they're not good."

Pasta

Homemade Pasta

Homemade Pasta with Fava Beans

Rigatoni with Broccoli

Orecchiette with Cauliflower

Penne with Escarole and Beans

Homemade Pasta or Spaghetti with
Cucuzza Longa (Sicilian Squash)

Ziti with Eggplant

Linguini with Marinara Sauce

Baked Ziti

Linguini with Garlic and Oil

Penne with Vodka Sauce

Penne with Pesto Sauce

Spaghetti Puttanesca

Linguini Finocchio con Sarde
(Linguini with Fennel and Sardines)

Homemade Pasta

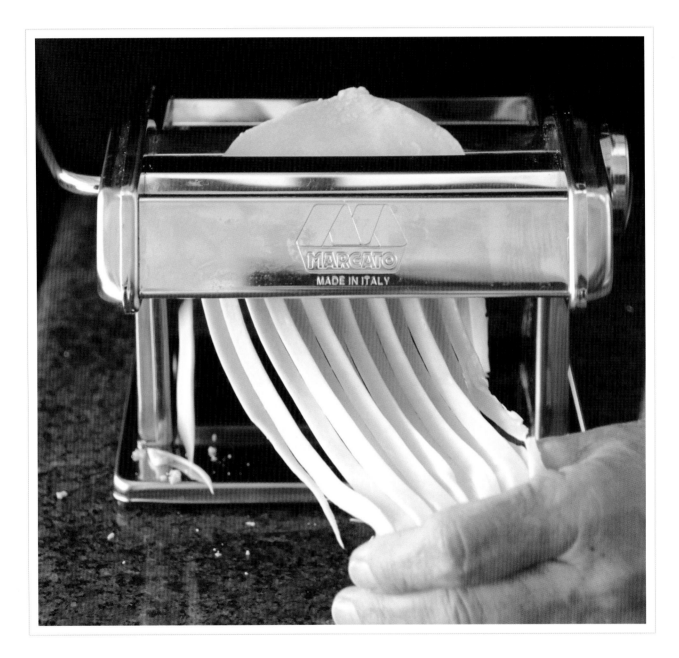

My mother, Elizabeth, made light, delicious pasta. She, of course, learned from her mother, and now I make pasta to honor her and our Sicilian heritage. I also make it because homemade pasta makes every sauce taste so much better! With practice, this wonderful and satisfying task will become second nature to you.

Make the Dough:
On a hard work surface, mound:

5 cups flour

Make a well in the center of the mound. Into the well in the center of the mound, break:

5 eggs

Beat the eggs with a fork. When the eggs are well beaten, use the fork to slowly draw in the flour and mix it into the liquid. At some point, you will use your hands to incorporate the eggs and flour. Add:

just enough water to make it into a heavy dough

Knead the Dough:
Flour the work surface. Knead the dough by holding it in place with the palm of one hand and stretching it away from itself with the other. Fold it together and repeat this maneuver until the dough is elastic and smooth. Cover and let rest (for 20 minutes).

Roll the Dough:
If you are working with a hand-cranked pasta machine, cut off a piece of dough. Feed it through the rollers of the machine set on the widest opening. Continue to set the machine on smaller rollers with each pass of the dough. It will get longer and longer. When the dough is the thickness of a dime, lay it on a kitchen towel to dry. After 15 minutes, turn the pasta strips to allow the second side to dry a bit. Be careful, though, because weather plays a big part in pasta making. If the day is hot, be careful not to let the pasta dry out too much.

Cut the Dough:
Add the cutting blade to the machine. Cut the strips of pasta to desired lengths and pass them through the machine.

Homemade Pasta
with Fava Beans

Every year my brother Ross planted dried fava beans from the previous year's crop. He planted them in the fall so that the new crop would be ready for our mother's birthday on March 19th. This was a cherished tradition in our family. My mother was always delighted to see the first fava beans. (If you cannot find fresh fava beans, look for frozen fava beans in Middle Eastern food stores.)

Prepare:
> **4 cups shelled fava beans**

Fava beans have outer pods which are approximately 8-9 inches long. Open the long pods and remove the fava beans. The fava beans have a smooth outer covering that is not edible, and has to be removed. My mother called this covering a "jacket." I like to remove the "jackets" with a sharp paring knife. Another method is to steam the fava beans to make the outer covering soft and easy to remove.

In a stock pot, heat:
> **3 Tablespoons oil**

Add and sauté until translucent:
> **6 spring onions, chopped (white and green parts)**

Add and stir to coat with oil:
> **the fava beans**

Add, bring to a simmer, and cook (for 30 minutes):
> **8 cups chicken broth**

Add:
> **fennel fronds, minced**
> **salt and pepper to taste**

While the beans are cooking, bring to a boil in a separate pot:
water for the pasta
1 Tablespoon salt

If you choose not to make homemade pasta but, instead, use a store-bought pasta like Barilla, break spaghetti into small pieces. If you are using homemade pasta, use the finest blade when you are rolling it out, and cut into short lengths before cooking.

Cook according to directions:
1 pound of pasta

When the pasta is done, use a strainer to scoop out the pasta and add it to the fava mixture.

Pour a bit of olive oil on top of the soup, and ladle it into bowls. Serve with:
freshly grated Parmigiano-Reggiano cheese

IL BUON GIORNO SI VEDE DAL
MATTINO.

"You recognize the good day early in the morning."
Good character is readily recognized.

Nine Centuries of Parmigiano-Reggiano Cheese

Parmigiano-Reggiano cheese has been around for a long time—nine centuries, in fact. It reached its peak between 1200-1300 AD and has remained popular ever since. Because generations of cheese makers have handed down their land, as well as their time-tested cultivation and processing techniques, to their families, this remarkable cheese has retained its purity, artful flavor, and texture. Today's modern cheese producers continue their ancestors' honored traditions with pride.

THE DIFFERENCE BETWEEN PECORINO-ROMANO AND PARMIGIANO-REGGIANO?

Parmigiano is noted for its nutty flavor, while Romano is considered more robust. Whichever one you choose is simply a matter of taste.

Rigatoni with Broccoli

This traditional pasta marries olive oil, garlic, broccoli, and cheese.

Prepare the Broccoli:
3 bunches of broccoli, cut into florets

In a large pot big enough to hold all the ingredients (the broccoli and the pasta), add and heat:
¼ cup olive oil

Add and cook over medium heat (for about 2 minutes):
6 cloves garlic, thinly sliced
pinch of crushed red pepper

Add, and cook the prepared broccoli, stirring occasionally (for 5 minutes or until the broccoli is coated with oil):
pinch of salt

Add and simmer (for 20 minutes):
4 cups chicken broth (preferably homemade)

Prepare the Pasta:
Bring a large pot of water (4 quarts) to a boil (if you cover it, the water will boil faster) and add:
1 Tablespoon salt
1 pound rigatoni

Stir the pasta so it does not stick together. Return to a boil, and cook uncovered according to package directions (usually 10-11 minutes).

Assemble the Dish:
Scoop the cooked pasta into the broccoli pot and let cook (for an additional 5 minutes).

Serve with:
½ cup freshly grated Pecorino-Romano or Parmigiano-Reggiano cheese

Orecchiette with Cauliflower

The word Orecchiette comes from orecchio (ear) and etto (small). It is a variety of homemade pasta typical of the Puglia or Apulia regions of Southern Italy. The shape of this pasta scoops and holds the delicious cheesy cauliflower mixture.

Prepare:
> **1 large head cauliflower**

Cut off the florets, and peel and cut the stems into pieces.

In a large pot over high heat, heat to boiling:
> **water**
> **2 teaspoons salt**

Add and cook until tender:
> **the cauliflower**

Scoop the cauliflower out of the water with a slotted spoon and put aside, saving the water.

In a frying pan over medium heat, heat:
> **¼ cup olive oil**

Add and cook:
> **3 cloves garlic, minced**

Slide the cauliflower into the pan and fry, mashing it in the pan as it cooks.

Prepare the Pasta:
In the pot with the saved cauliflower water, add and cook until done:
> **½ pound orecchiette pasta**

Assemble the Dish:

When the pasta is cooked, scoop the pasta into the frying pan with the cauliflower, and toss. Add a little of the pasta water to the mixture to make it soupy.

Serve with:
freshly grated Parmigiano-Reggiano cheese

As a Baked Casserole:

To make this dish as a baked casserole, assemble the ingredients in a bowl, add, and mix well:
½ cup mozzarella cheese

Turn into a casserole dish and top with:
½ cup grated Parmesan cheese

Bake at 350° (for 30 minutes).

I GUAI DELLA "PIGNATA" LI SA LA CUCCHIAIA CHE LI "RIMINA."

"Only the stirring spoon knows the troubles of the pot."

The Rainbow of Cauliflower Colors

White, of course, is the variety most often used.

Orange is a Canadian variant that contains more vitamin A.

Green, also called "Romanesco Broccoli," has a spiky head.

Purple contains *anthocyanins*, an antioxidant similar to that found in red cabbage and red wine.

Fresh cauliflower is a summer favorite. While it is available year-round in grocery stores, there is nothing quite like a freshly picked cauliflower from your local farmer's market.

Penne with Escarole and Beans

Escarole, or broad-leaved endive (var latifolia) has broad, pale green leaves.

Wash well and place into a colander to drain:
> **1 head escarole, sliced thinly**

In a large pan, heat:
> **¼ cup olive oil**

Add and sauté until slightly golden:
> **6 cloves garlic, thinly sliced**

Add to the pan and stir:
> **the escarole**

Pour in and cook (for 20 minutes):
> **4 cups chicken broth**

Add and heat through:
> **2 cans (15 oz.) cannellini beans**
> **red pepper flakes and salt and pepper to taste**

Prepare the Pasta:
Bring a large pot of water (4 quarts) to a boil (cover it so the water will boil faster) and add:
> **1 Tablespoon salt**
> **½ pound penne or short pasta**

Stir the pasta so it does not stick together. Return to a boil and cook uncovered according to package directions (usually 11-12 minutes).

Assemble the Dish:
Scoop the cooked pasta into the escarole mixture, and stir to combine. Use some pasta water to make it soupier, if desired.

Serve with: **freshly grated Parmigiano-Reggiano cheese**

Homemade Pasta or Spaghetti with Cucuzza Longa (Sicilian Squash)

Cucuzza longa is a variety of squash (reaching 2-3 feet long) grown on trellises in the summer. My father, however, always picked them when they were shorter and more tender. They can be found in Italian markets or in an older Italian's garden.

In a pot, heat:
>	**¼ cup olive oil**

Add and cook until translucent:
>	**6 scallions or spring onions, chopped (green stem included)**

Season with:
>	**salt and pepper**

Add to the pot and cook until the squash is tender (about 30 minutes):
>	**1 or 2 cucuzzi (depending on size), peeled and cubed**
>	**2 cups chicken broth (preferably homemade)**

Prepare the Pasta:
Bring a large pot of water (4 quarts) to a boil (cover it so the water will boil faster) and add:
>	**1 Tablespoon salt**
>	**½ pound homemade pasta or packaged spaghetti, broken into pieces**

Stir the pasta so it does not stick together, return to a boil, and cook uncovered according to package directions (usually 10-11 minutes).

Assemble the Dish:
Scoop the cooked pasta into the squash sauce and stir to combine. You can use some of the pasta water to make the dish soupy.

Season with:
>	**salt and pepper to taste**

Serve with:
>	**freshly grated Parmigiano-Reggiano cheese**

Zita with Eggplant

My mother made great bread and pasta, but she was not the star in our kitchen. My father was the accomplished cook, and he did all the serious cooking in our house. Fortunately, he was creative and innovative and used the bounty from his garden. He made this pasta dish when beautiful purple eggplants were in season.

In a deep skillet, heat:
> **½ cup olive oil**

Add and sauté until golden (about 10 minutes):
> **2 eggplants, cut into 1-inch cubes**

Pour into the skillet and cook over medium (for 30 minutes):
> **1 28-oz. can crushed tomatoes**
> **½ teaspoon red pepper flakes**
> **1 teaspoon sugar**
> **salt and pepper to taste**

Prepare the Pasta:
Bring a large pot of water (4 quarts) to a boil (if you cover it, the water will boil faster) and add:
> **1 Tablespoon salt**
> **1 pound ziti pasta**

Stir the pasta so it does not stick together, return to a boil, and cook uncovered according to package directions (usually 10-11 minutes).

Assemble the Dish:
Drain the pasta well and add to the sauce. Sprinkle with:
> **freshly grated Parmigiano-Reggiano cheese**

Linguini with Marinara Sauce

This is an easy sauce to make and a mainstay because it can be used in many dishes: as a pizza topping, with chicken Parmesan and lasagna, and as an accompaniment to chicken cutlets, fried calamari, or grilled vegetables … you get the idea. It also makes a great quick and satisfying meal.

Prepare the Pasta:
Bring a large pot of water (4 quarts) to a boil (if you cover it, the water will boil faster) and add:

> **1 Tablespoon salt**
> **1 pound linguini pasta**

Stir the pasta so it does not stick together, return to a boil, and cook uncovered according to package directions (usually 8-10 minutes).

While you are waiting for the water to boil, make the sauce.

Prepare the Sauce:
In a stovetop skillet (large enough to hold the pasta when it is cooked), heat:

> **⅓ cup olive oil**

Add and sauté (for a minute or two):

> **3-5 cloves garlic, chopped**
> **½ teaspoon crushed red pepper, or to taste**

Carefully add, and cook until the pasta is ready:

> **1 28-oz. can crushed tomatoes**
> **1 teaspoon sugar**
> **1 teaspoon dried oregano or 1 Tablespoon fresh chopped oregano**

Assemble the Dish:
Combine the sauce with the linguini and mix well.

Serve with:

> **freshly grated Parmigiano-Reggiano cheese**

Baked Ziti

This is a great party dish. It can be prepared ahead of time, and it feeds a crowd.

Prepare the Sauce:
In a very large saucepan, heat over medium:
> **¼ cup olive oil**

Add and sauté until translucent:
> **1 onion, chopped finely**
> **3 cloves garlic, minced**

Pour in and cook (for 30 minutes):
> **2 28-oz. cans crushed tomatoes**
> **1 Tablespoon oregano**
> **1 teaspoon sugar and salt and pepper to taste**

Prepare the Pasta:
Bring a large pot of water (4 quarts) to a boil (cover it so the water will boil faster) and add:
> **1 Tablespoon salt**
> **1 pound ziti pasta**

Stir the pasta so it does not stick together, return to a boil, and cook uncovered until slightly undercooked (about 7-9 minutes). It will continue to cook in the oven.

Assemble the Dish:
In a 9x13 baking pan, ladle enough sauce to cover the bottom. Spoon half the pasta over the sauce and sprinkle with:
> **½ pound grated mozzarella cheese (you will need another ¼ pound later)**
> **½ cup grated Parmigiano-Reggiano cheese (save another ¼ cup later)**

Dot with spoons of:
> **half of a 15-oz. container of ricotta cheese**

Repeat the layers, and sprinkle the top with mozzarella and parmesan cheese. Bake at 350° (for 45 minutes).

Linguini with Garlic and Oil

This dish is quick, easy, and very tasty!

Prepare the Pasta:

Bring a large pot of water (4 quarts) to a boil (if you cover it, the water will boil faster) and add:

1 Tablespoon salt
½ pound linguini or spaghetti

Stir the pasta so it does not stick together, return to a boil, and cook uncovered according to package directions (usually 8-10 minutes).

While the pasta is cooking, in a large skillet heat:

½ cup olive oil

Add:

6 cloves garlic, thinly sliced
salt and pepper to taste
¼ teaspoon red pepper flakes

Lower heat to medium and cook until light brown. Remove the pan from the heat.

Assemble the Dish:

If the sauce has cooled, return the skillet with the sauce to a low heat.
Drain the pasta and add it to the skillet. Toss until the pasta is well coated with the sauce.

Sprinkle with:

grated Parmigiano-Reggiano cheese
1 Tablespoon flat-leaf parsley, chopped

Penne with
Vodka Sauce

Grapevines and Olive Branches

An all-time favorite recipe for special occasions.

In a large saucepan, melt and heat:
1 stick unsalted butter

Add and sauté until translucent (about 5 minutes):
3 cloves garlic, peeled and finely chopped

Pour in and cook (for an additional 5 minutes):
½ cup vodka

Add and cook (for 5 minutes):
½ cup basil, finely chopped

Add and cook (for 30-45 minutes):
1 28-oz. can of whole tomatoes, liquefied

Prepare the Pasta:
Bring a large pot of water (4 quarts) to a boil (if you cover it, the water will boil faster) and add:
1 Tablespoon salt
1 pound of penne

Stir the pasta so it does not stick together, return to a boil, and cook uncovered according to package directions (usually 11-12 minutes).

10 minutes before the pasta is done, add to the sauce, and heat over medium heat:
1 cup heavy cream

Assemble the Dish:
To serve, ladle the sauce over the pasta, and garnish with a basil leaf.

Serve with:
freshly grated Parmigiano-Reggiano cheese

Penne with
Pesto Sauce

Pesto is a sauce that originated in Genoa in the Liguria region of Northern Italy. The name comes from the Genoese word pestâ (Italian: pestare), which means to pound or to crush, in reference to the original method of preparing pesto with a marble mortar and wooden pestle.

In a blender, place:

2 cups fresh basil leaves
½ cup pignoli nuts (pine nuts), lightly toasted
3 cloves garlic
½ cup olive oil
½ cup grated Parmesan cheese

Pulse until the pesto is smooth.

Prepare the Pasta:
Bring a large pot of water (4 quarts) to a boil (if you cover it, the water will boil faster) and add:

1 Tablespoon salt
1 pound penne or other short pasta

Stir the pasta so it does not stick together, return to a boil, and cook uncovered according to package directions (usually 11-12 minutes). Drain the pasta.

Assemble the Dish:
Toss the pesto with the pasta and mix until well coated.

Spaghetti Puttanesca

In Italian, spaghetti puttanesca literally means "spaghetti a la whore." It is a tangy, somewhat salty, Italian pasta dish invented in the mid-twentieth century.

In a skillet large enough to hold the sauce and the cooked pasta, heat:
⅓ cup olive oil

Add and sauté over low heat until garlic is golden:
3 cloves garlic, finely chopped
½ Tablespoon red pepper flakes

Raise the heat to medium. Add and cook (for 15-20 minutes or until the sauce is thickened):
1 28-oz. can peeled and chopped tomatoes, drained, or 2½ pounds fresh tomatoes, peeled and chopped
1 teaspoon dried oregano
pinch of salt

Stir in, and continue cooking (for 5 minutes):
½ cup pitted Kalamata or black Italian olives
¼ cup capers
3 anchovy fillets
¼ cup fresh parsley, chopped

Prepare the Pasta:
Bring a large pot of water (4 quarts) to a boil (if you cover it, the water will boil faster) and add:
1 Tablespoon salt
1 pound spaghetti

Stir the pasta so it does not stick together, return to a boil, and cook uncovered according to package directions (usually 10-12 minutes).

Assemble the Dish:
Drain the pasta and add it to the simmering sauce. Toss well and enjoy.

Linguini Finocchio con Sarde
(Linguini with Fennel and Sardines)

My father, Vincent, had many fishermen friends in San Diego. Once, he had helped them get a fishing boat back from the Mexican government after it had been confiscated for being in restricted waters. The fishermen were grateful and returned his kindness by supplying him with seasonal fish. The following is a traditional dish served for the Feast of St. Joseph on March 19th—my mother's birthday.

In a deep pot, heat:
> **¼ cup olive oil**

Add and sauté until wilted:
> **1 large onion, chopped**
> **3 cloves garlic, minced**

Stir in and break up with a wooden spoon:
> **1 pound fresh sardines (cleaned of heads, insides, and fins),**
> **cut into bite-sized pieces**

When the sardines are no longer pink, pour in and cook on medium (for 30 minutes):
> **1 28-oz. can of tomatoes, pureed**

Add and allow to cook (for an additional 30 minutes):
> **1 fennel bulb (preferably wild), minced**
> **fennel fronds, chopped**
> **⅓ cup pignoli nuts (pine nuts)**
> **⅓ cup golden raisins**

In the meantime, add to a frying pan and heat:
> **¼ cup olive oil**

Add and sauté until golden (watch carefully because they burn easily):
> **1 cup dry bread crumbs**

Prepare according to directions on the package, and drain:
> **1 pound linguini pasta**

At this time, you can pour the sauce over the drained pasta and sprinkle with the sautéed bread crumbs, or you can pour the cooked pasta into a baking dish and top with the sauce and bread crumbs and bake at 350° (for 30 minutes).

The dried bread crumbs are called modica. *Some Sicilians are opposed to using cheese with fish dishes; instead, they use modica for the finishing touch.*

IL PANE DIVISO É LA SALUTE DEI DENTI.

"Bread that is broken in pieces is healthy for the teeth."
A separate household for the newlywed prevents family quarrels.

Bread

My Mother's Braided Rolls

Panelli

Pane Consado (Fixed Bread)

My Mother's Braided Rolls

This recipe makes about 24 rolls, depending on how large you make them.

My Mother's Original Bread Recipe:
   5 pounds flour
   3 packets of dry yeast
   handful of salt (about ¼ cup)
   handful of sugar (about ¼ cup)

Make the Dough:
Put the yeast in 2 cups of warm water and wait until it starts to foam. Pour the yeast onto the dry ingredients. Mix it by hand. Add more water, if necessary. Knead until smooth.

Divide the dough in half and place in mixer bowl with dough hook. Process until smooth. Prepare the second batch the same way. Knead both halves together by hand until smooth.

Place dough in a large bowl. Cover with plastic wrap and then a towel. Let it rise until doubled (1-1½ hours). Punch the dough down, cover again, and let rise another hour.

Turn the dough out onto a smooth surface.

(*At this point, my mother cut a small cross on top of the dough, kissed her fingers, and put the kiss on the little etched cross. This was her way of giving thanks for the gift of the bread.*)

Form the Braided Rolls:
Divide the dough into two halves. Divide each half into 12 equal size pieces, making a total of 24 rolls. Toss each piece in your hands until it is a rope about 1-inch diameter (about 12 inches long). Take one end and loop it around to form a U. Starting at the bottom of the U, twist the two ropes together and have the two ends meet. Press the two ends together.

Put the bread knots onto a greased baking sheet, and let rise 1 hour, covered, in a warm place. Before baking, dampen each roll with a little water, and sprinkle with:
   sesame seeds

Bake at 350° (for 30 minutes or until golden brown).

Panelli

🍇 Grapevines and Olive Branches

When my mother made bread, she frequently took a small portion of the dough after it had risen once and made panelli, a wonderful afternoon treat.

Roll pieces of the dough (see above recipe) into balls about the size of a golf ball.

With a rolling pin, roll into small circles about 3-4 inches in diameter.

Fry the dough circles until golden brown in:
> **olive oil**

Sprinkle circles with:
> **sugar**
> **cinnamon**

METTI IL PANE AL DENTE, LA FAME SI RISENTE.

"Bread touching the teeth sparks one's hunger."
See an old lover and our love is rekindled.

Pane Consado
(Fixed Bread)

I frequently make Pane Consado for guests. My father liked his with a few filets of anchovy.

Take hot bread out of the oven.

Slice bread in half and sprinkle with:
> **olive oil**
> **fresh grated cheese**
> **black pepper**

Italian Bread Making

For centuries, bread has been a stable grain throughout the world. In Italy, after new wheat milling techniques were discovered and implemented, bread making became an art. The first Roman baking school opened in the first century AD.

Here are a few well-known Italian breads:

Cecìna: The primary ingredient in this Tuscan coast flat bread is chickpea flour, which adds extra protein and depth of flavor.

Ciabatta: A popular bread often used for sandwiches and spreads. Originating in the area of Liguria (a coastal region in northwestern Italy), it is flat and porous with a crisp crust.

Fragguno: This festive bread is often eaten in Calabria (a region of southern Italy) on Good Friday and Easter Sunday.

Panettone: A soft, sweet bread native to Milan that is often served on Christmas day. It can be used as a base for bread puddings.

Taralli: A savory snack food, like a bread stick or pretzel, that is common throughout southern Italy.

GALLINA VECCHIA FA BUON BRODO.

"An old hen makes the best soup."
An older girl might be a better catch!

Meat & Poultry

Ross's Lamb and Fava Bean Stew

Spedini

Sausage with Peppers and Onions

Chicken Cutlets

Sautéed Broccoli Rabe with Sausage

Chicken Cacciatore

Roasted Leg of Lamb

Amogue (Steak Sauce)

Braciola

Meatballs

Sunday Tomato Sauce with Meats

Ross's Lamb and Fava Bean Stew

In Sicily, the 19th of March is celebrated as "La Festa di San Giuseppe." This day of celebration has religious origins; it honors Saint Joseph. La Festa di San Giuseppe illustrates how each festival is connected with a specific type of cuisine. Legend has it that Saint Joseph saved Sicily from a famine and that the fava bean crop relieved the pain of the population. Hence, the fava bean forms an integral part of the food for the day. We always had fava beans at the Winery. We harvested them in late spring. After the harvest, the workers laid the plants out on concrete to let them dry out in the sun. When the plants were perfectly dry, the workers smashed the pods, picked out the fava beans, and put them in buckets so we could use them during the winter.

Since the "jackets" on the dried fava beans were very dry, they had to be soaked overnight to loosen the outer skin. Fava beans have a couple of layers of skin. You can use a knife or your fingers to remove the skin. Once the skin is removed, the beans are ready to be cooked. On cold winter days, my brother, Ross, used to make this stew in a large cauldron in his fireplace.

In a heavy stew pot over medium heat, heat:
> **¼ cup olive oil**

Add and sauté until translucent:
> **1 large onion, chopped**
> **6 cloves garlic, chopped**

Add and cook until browned (about 10 minutes):
> **1 pound cubed lamb (or another meat of your choice)**

Add, bring to a boil, and simmer (for 1 hour):
3 cups fava beans (Dried fava beans can be purchased in many Mexican or Middle Eastern markets.)
> **1 cup peas**
> **2 bay leaves**
> **enough water to cover**
> **salt and pepper to taste**

Spedini

Every Sicilian cook has his or her own recipe for spedini. This was my father's recipe, and now it is mine. Spedini is a family favorite and is always very well received. We use freshly picked lemons from the Winery to make this dish. Spedini is a great dish to make with many helping hands. It is a little bit of work, but it's well worth the effort. The tang of the lemon and the flavor of the bay leaves work very well together.

In a large bowl, combine:
> **2 cups lemon juice**
> **2 cups olive oil**

Drop into the lemon-oil mixture and marinate (for at least 2 hours):
> **2 large London broil steaks, sliced across the grain into ¼-inch slices**

1 Hour Before Dinner:
In a large bowl, combine:
> **4 cups dried bread crumbs**
> **½ cup parsley, chopped**
> **3 cloves garlic, pressed**
> **salt and pepper to taste**

Coat each slice of meat with the bread crumb mixture, and roll up jelly-roll style.

Gather together the following:
> **skewers**
> **wedges of onion**
> **fresh bay leaves**

Skewer the meat onto the stick, add a fresh bay leaf, a single wedge of onion, and repeat until the skewer is filled.

Drizzle the marinade over the skewers and grill until browned.

Sausage with Peppers
and Onions

What is referred to as Italian sausage (salsiccia in Italian) is most often a style of pork sausage that uses fennel and/or anise as its primary seasoning. In Italy, however, there is a wide variety of sausages to pick from. The two most common are hot/sweet and sweet/mild, the primary difference being the hot red pepper flakes that are added to the spice mix of the former. Choose the flavor of sausage that appeals to you most. The large quantity of peppers and onions in this recipe absorb some of the spiciness of the hot sausage while adding a lot of flavor.

In a deep skillet, heat:
> **1 Tablespoon olive oil**

Add and brown:
> **12 Italian sausages**

When the sausages are cooked, remove them to a baking pan with deep sides.

In the same skillet, add and heat:
> **2 Tablespoons olive oil**

Add and sauté over medium heat until limp and slightly brown:
> **4 large onions, sliced**
> **6 green bell peppers, sliced**
> **salt and pepper to taste**

Place the onions and peppers on top of the sausage, cover the pan with foil, and bake at 350° (for 30 minutes). Uncover the pan, and continue baking (for an additional 15 minutes).

Serve with Italian rolls for sandwiches, or use as a first course.

Chicken Cutlets

Chicken cutlets are a family favorite that can be eaten hot or cold (if any are left over). They were always available in my parents' refrigerator.

Cut in half horizontally (to make 8 cutlets):
4 chicken breasts, boneless and skinless

Cover with plastic wrap and pound to an even ½ inch thickness. Pat dry and sprinkle with:
salt and pepper

In a pie plate, place:
¾ cup flour

In a second pie plate, beat with a fork:
2 eggs

In a third pie plate, prepare the bread crumbs by combining and mixing well:
1 cup dried bread crumbs
2 cloves garlic, smashed
½ cup Italian parsley, chopped
½ cup freshly grated Parmigiano-Reggiano cheese

Dredge each chicken breast in the flour, making sure to coat both sides. Shake off the excess flour, and then dip into the beaten egg. Finally, roll the chicken in the bread crumb mixture. Transfer to a wire rack and let the breaded cutlets sit (for 5 minutes).

In a large frying pan, heat:
⅓ cup vegetable oil (or more)

Fry the chicken in batches over medium-high heat until golden, being careful not to crowd the pan. You can keep the cooked chicken warm in a 200° oven while you continue cooking the other batches.

Serve with:
lemon wedges

Sautéed Broccoli Rabe
with Sausage

Broccoli Rabe has many names, such as rapini or broccoli raab. In Italy it is called "cime di rapa," which literally means "turnip tops." In Naples it is referred to as "friarielli;" and in Portugal and Spain it is called, "grelos."

Broccoli Rabe is a healthy alternative to a green cruciferous vegetable. The leaves, buds, and stems are edible. The buds somewhat resemble broccoli but don't actually form a large head. Broccoli rabe has a nutty, slightly bitter, and pungent taste that balances and lightens the stronger flavors of the link sausage in this classic recipe.

Prepare:
> **1 pound broccoli rabe**

Trim the broccoli, cut off the stem ends, wash well in cool water, and cut into bite-sized pieces.

In a large pot, heat:
> **3 Tablespoons olive oil**

Add and cook over medium heat until sausage is done:
> **4 links of Italian sausage, cut into 1-inch pieces**
> **3 garlic cloves, thinly sliced**
> **½ cup black Italian olives**
> **pinch of crushed red pepper**

Add and stir well:
> **broccoli rabe**
> **salt to taste**

Cover the pot and cook until the broccoli rabe is tender (about 15 minutes).

Serve hot or at room temperature.

Chicken Cacciatore

This is a rustic, hardy, and satisfying dish. "Cacciatore" means "hunter" in Italian.

Rinse and pat dry:
> **2 3-pound chickens, cut into pieces**

In a Dutch oven over medium heat, heat:
> **2 Tablespoons oil**

Add the chicken pieces, skin side down. Sprinkle with:
> **salt and pepper to taste**

Sauté chicken (for 10 minutes on each side), and remove to a platter.

In the same Dutch oven, over medium heat, heat:
> **2 Tablespoons oil**

Add and cook, stirring frequently, until the vegetables are tender and lightly browned (about 15 minutes):
> **3 red bell peppers, seeded and cut into narrow strips**
> **1 large onion, thinly sliced**
> **16 oz. mushrooms, trimmed and halved**

Stir in and cook (for 2 minutes):
> **6 garlic cloves, halved**

Add, bring to a simmer, and transfer Dutch oven to the pre-heated oven:
> **2 28-oz. cans Italian peeled tomatoes, chopped**
> **2 teaspoons oregano, dried**
> **salt and pepper to taste**
> **the chicken pieces**

Cover and bake at 350°(for 1 hour).

Serve with pasta or rice.

Roasted Leg of Lamb

Eating lamb on Easter is part of the Italian culture, history, and tradition. Lamb is symbolic in many regions and religions, and the custom of eating lamb on special occasions goes back thousands of years, especially in the areas around the Mediterranean Sea.

In a large roasting pan, place:
> **1 bone-in leg of lamb (4-5 pounds)**

Pierce the top all over with the sharp point of a knife. Into each slit, push in:
> **1 thin slice of garlic (total of 5-6 cloves of garlic, thinly sliced)**
> **several rosemary leaves (total of 3-4 sprigs of rosemary)**

Once you have finished stuffing all the slits, drizzle over the top of the lamb:
> **olive oil**
> **salt and pepper**

Around the lamb, at the bottom of the roasting pan, add:
> **3 onions, sliced into thick rings**
> **6 potatoes, quartered**

Roast the lamb at 400° to seal (for 15 minutes), then turn the temperature down to 350° and continue cooking until the meat thermometer registers 150° for medium (about one hour).

Watch the vegetables carefully, and remove to a plate if they are browning too much.

Before carving, let lamb rest (for 10 minutes).

Amogue
(Steak Sauce)

Whenever we barbecued steaks at home (which was often), my dad made Amogu. He dipped a branch of rosemary into the Amogu and brushed it onto the steaks as they were grilling. So delicious! And the aromas from the garlic, tomatoes, and rosemary are incredible.

In a large mortar, pound the following with a pestle until it becomes a paste:

6-8 cloves garlic
1 Tablespoon salt

Add and continue to pound until the tomatoes are chunky and give off some juice:

3-4 large tomatoes, peeled, seeded, and chopped

Add and continue mixing:

ground black pepper, to taste
1 cup olive oil

Season the steaks by brushing them with the sauce using:

large branch of fresh rosemary

INTERESTING FACT

Amogue (a-mo-jio)
This is an authentic Sicilian sauce (especially good made fresh from garden, sun-ripened on the vine, tomatoes.)

IF YOU HAVE LEFTOVER SAUCE, USE IT
- as a bruschetta topping
- as a dipping sauce for bread
- for any grilled meat or fish

Braciola

Braciola, a traditional Italian dish, literally means "meat roasted over live coals."

Prepare Steak:

1 pound round steak, cut about ¼-inch thick into 4 pieces of meat weighing about ¼ pound each (Pound each piece of meat between two pieces of wax paper to form equally sized rectangles.)

Rub meat with:

a garlic clove

In a bowl, place and mix together:

2 oz. caciocavallo or provolone cheese, diced
2 oz. Sicilian or Italian hard salami, diced
½ cup fresh bread crumbs
3 Tablespoons pignoli nuts (pine nuts)
2 Tablespoons flat-leaf parsley, chopped
1 egg, beaten

Divide the mixture into 4 equal portions.

Cover the center section of the pounded meat with the mixture, and add to the middle:

3 slices of hard boiled egg for each slice of meat (about 3 eggs total)

Roll the meat slices up jelly-roll style, and tie with kitchen string.

In a skillet over medium heat, heat:

¼ cup olive oil

Add the meat rolls and fry on all sides until browned and slightly crispy.

Discard any remaining olive oil. Return the braciola to the pan and add:

tomato sauce to cover, preferably homemade

Bring to a boil, lower heat and simmer (for 30 minutes).

Meatballs

Most families have their own prized meatball recipe. This one has been a staple in our family for generations. Combining three meats, using fresh bread instead of breadcrumbs, and frying in olive oil make this recipe a timeless tradition. You can expect to make about 12 nice-sized meatballs.

Place in a large bowl and allow to soak (for 10 minutes), then mash slightly with a fork:

6 slices of white bread, crusts removed

milk, enough to cover the bread (½-¾ cup)

Add to the bowl and mix together:

1 pound ground meat, preferably a combination of ground beef, pork, and veal

3 large eggs

1 teaspoon garlic, finely minced

½ cup freshly grated Pecorino-Romano or Parmigiano-Reggiano cheese

2 Tablespoons fresh flat-leaf parsley, finely chopped

1 teaspoon salt

freshly ground pepper

Divide mixture into 12 equal pieces and shape into 2½- to 3-inch balls.

In a large skillet, heat until very hot (but not smoking):

⅔ cup olive oil

Brown meatballs on all sides (5-7 minutes). Remove from pan and drain on a paper towel.

Sunday Tomato Sauce
with Meats

This hearty Sunday meal is often referred to as "Sunday Gravy." It calls up wonderful memories of Italian-American family dinners across the country. In essence, this dish is a rich tomato-based sauce with a variety of meats. It is often served with pasta. The meats added to the tomato sauce could include some or all of the following: braciola, homemade meatballs, spareribs, Italian sausage, lean beef, and lean pork.

Prepare and Assemble the Meats:
  meatballs (see previous recipe)
  braciola (see previous recipe)

In a large, heavy pot over medium heat, heat:
  2 Tablespoons olive oil

Add and cook, turning occasionally (for about 15 minutes or until browned on all sides):
  1 pound meaty pork spareribs, patted dry

Transfer pork to a plate.

To the same pot, add and brown on all sides:
  1 pound Italian-style plain or fennel pork sausages

Set the sausages aside with the pork.

Make the Sauce:
  In the same pot, sauté until translucent:
  1 onion, chopped fine

Add and cook until fragrant:
  4 cloves garlic, minced

Add and stir to combine:

6 basil leaves, torn into small pieces
1 teaspoon oregano
salt and pepper to taste

Add and then cook over medium heat (for 30 minutes):

4 28- to 35-oz. cans Italian peeled tomatoes, crushed in a blender
1 Tablespoon sugar
1 small can of tomato paste

Add to the sauce and continue cooking (for 1 hour):

the spareribs
the sausage

After one hour, gently nestle into the sauce:

the meatballs
the braciola

Continue to simmer (for 30 minutes or until cooked through).

Serve with:

at least 1 pound of pasta (your choice), cooked according to directions
freshly grated Pecorino-Romano or Parmigiano-Reggiano cheese

History of Tomato Sauce in Italy

It is a misconception that the humble tomato has always been central to Italian cuisine. The tomato was introduced to European botanists in the sixteenth century by returning Spanish conquistadors.

Italian pasta sauce varieties:

Acciughe: Contains anchovies, garlic, oil, and parsley.

Aglio e olio: This typical Italian aioli sounds fancy but is simply a flavored mayonnaise.

Alfredo: One of the more beloved cream sauces. It is most often served over fettuccine.

Bolognese: A rich meat sauce that goes well with any type of meat or pasta and is usually flavored with red wine (although some recipes call for white wine). The type of wine used depends on where in Italy the recipe originated. This sauce can include vegetables and a touch of nutmeg.

Burro: A simple butter sauce with grated Parmesan cheese.

Cacciatore: A distinctive meat sauce often flavored with juniper.

Marinara: A traditional everyday sauce of fresh tomatoes, olive oil, garlic, and basil.

Pesto: A sauce made with nuts (pine nuts are traditional, but other nuts can be used). It most often contains oil, grated cheese, fresh basil (or similar herb), and garlic pounded into a thick, rich paste.

Romana: A meat or chicken sauce that contains chopped mushrooms.

Tartufata: A unique, rustic truffle sauce often flavored with red or white wine and garlic.

Vongole: A traditional clam sauce made with onions, tomatoes, olive oil, and garlic.

IL PESCE PUZZA DALLA TESTA.

"An old fish smells from the head down."
Certain groups smell from the top echelon down.

Fish & Seafood

Rollatine di Pesce Spada (Grilled Swordfish Rolls)

Swordfish Rolls in Tomato Sauce

Insalata di Mare (Seafood Salad)

Tuna Salad with Oil and Lemon

Rollatine di Pesce Spada
(Grilled Swordfish Rolls)

For this recipe, prepare a medium to hot fire in a charcoal grill, or preheat a gas grill or broiler. Place the grill rack or broiler pan 4 inches from the heat source.

Prepare:
> **1½ pounds swordfish, skin removed and cut into very thin slices**

Place the swordfish slices between two sheets of plastic wrap. Using a meat mallet, gently pound the slices to an even ¼-inch thickness.

Prepare the Filling:
In a bowl, combine:

¾ cup plain bread crumbs	**1 large clove garlic, minced**
2 Tablespoons capers, chopped	**2 Tablespoons pignoli nuts**
2 Tablespoons fresh flat-leaf	**(pine nuts), chopped**
parsley, chopped	**2 Tablespoons golden raisins, chopped**

Add to the filling and mix until the crumbs are evenly moistened:
> **3 Tablespoons olive oil**

Assemble the Swordfish Rolls:
Place a Tablespoon of the crumb mixture at one narrow end of each piece of fish. Roll up the fish and fasten it closed with a toothpick.

In a small bowl, whisk together:
> **1 Tablespoon olive oil and 2 Tablespoons lemon juice**

Brush the mixture over the rolls, and sprinkle the fish with any remaining bread crumb mixture, patting it so it adheres.

Cook the Rolls:
Grill the rolls (for 3 to 4 minutes on each side, or until they are browned and feel firm when pressed in the center). They should be slightly rare.

Serve hot with: **lemon wedges**

Swordfish Rolls
in Tomato Sauce

Swordfish is a favorite of Southern Italians, especially in Sicily, where a general rule applies ... when cooking fish, leave the cheese out.

The swordfish rolls described in the previous recipe are the foundation of this dish.

Prepare:
1½ pounds swordfish, skin removed and cut into very thin slices

Place the swordfish slices between two sheets of plastic wrap. Using a meat mallet, gently pound the slices to an even ¼-inch thickness.

Prepare the Filling:
In a bowl, combine:
¾ cup plain bread crumbs
2 Tablespoons capers, chopped
2 Tablespoons fresh flat-leaf parsley, chopped
1 large clove garlic, minced
2 Tablespoons pignoli nuts (pine nuts), chopped
2 Tablespoons golden raisins, chopped

Add to the filling and mix until the crumbs are evenly moistened:
3 Tablespoons olive oil

Assemble the Swordfish Rolls:
Place a Tablespoon of the crumb mixture at one narrow end of each piece of fish. Roll up the fish and fasten it closed with a toothpick.

Sauté the rolls in olive oil in a large frying pan.

Prepare the Sauce:
In a stock pot, heat over medium:
¼ cup olive oil

Add and sauté until translucent:

1 onion, chopped finely
3 cloves garlic, minced

Pour in and cook (for 30 minutes):

2 28-oz. cans crushed tomatoes
1 Tablespoon oregano
1 teaspoon sugar
salt and pepper to taste

Add the sautéed swordfish rolls and simmer (for about 30 minutes).

Serve them over pasta, as you would meatballs.

About Swordfish

Swordfish are abundant in the waters around Sicily; therefore, there are many Sicilian swordfish recipes. Swordfish is a mild, firm white fish that can be used in many dishes, from carpaccio to rollatini to grilled swordfish steaks.

The fish markets in Sicily display the entire fish, sword and all. The fish monger cuts off any amount of fish the customer wants.

IL PIATTO NON SI RESTITUISCE VUOTO.

"It's an old custom never to return an empty dish."

Insalata di Mare
(Seafood Salad)

This is a refreshing seafood salad that combines crispy celery with bright citrus and briny olives.

Prepare the Mussels:
Cover with cold water and let rest (for 30 minutes):
> **2 pounds mussels**

Scrub the mussels with a stiff brush and scrape off any barnacles or seaweed. Discard any mussels with cracked shells or shells that do not shut tightly when tapped. Remove the beards by pulling them toward the narrow end of the shells.

Place the mussels in a large pot with 1 cup boiling water. Cover and cook until the mussels open (about 5-10 minutes). Discard any that do not open.

Prepare the Other Fish:
Bring a large saucepan of water to a simmer and add:
> **1 pound medium shrimp, shelled and de-veined**
> **salt to taste**

Cook until the shrimp are just cooked through (2 to 3 minutes). Scoop out the shrimp and cool.

In the same water used for the shrimp, drop:
> **1 pound cleaned calamari, cut crosswise into ½-inch rings**

Cook just until opaque (about 1 minute). Drain thoroughly and cool under cold running water.

Prepare the Dressing:

In a small bowl, whisk together:

> **⅓ cup extra virgin olive oil**
> **½ teaspoon lemon zest**
> **2 Tablespoons fresh lemon juice, or to taste**
> **2 Tablespoons fresh flat-leaf parsley, chopped**
> **2 cloves garlic, minced**
> **pinch of crushed red pepper**
> **salt to taste**

Assemble the Salad:

Place the seafood in a large bowl and add:

> **1 cup celery, thinly sliced**
> **1 lemon, thinly sliced**
> **1 cup pitted green olives, sliced**

Pour the dressing over the salad mixture and toss well.

Garnish with:

> **lemon wedges**

Lemons

We always serve fish on Christmas Eve. Some families believe that they should eat seven different fish on that date to represent the Seven Sacraments. Other families dine on twelve fish to represent the Twelve Apostles.

Our family still honors this tradition by making seven fish dishes.

THEY CAN INCLUDE:
- grilled swordfish
- frutti de mare salad
- pasta finocchio con sarde
- shrimp and mussels
- calamari and octopus
- pasta with clam sauce

Tuna Salad with Oil and Lemon

This is a simple, fresh recipe with lots of lemony goodness.

In a large pot big enough to accommodate the tuna pieces, bring to a boil:
water
2 Tablespoons salt

Add to the boiling water and boil (for 20-25 minutes):
2 pounds of fresh albacore tuna

Remove the tuna from the pot, drain it and allow it to cool.

Place the tuna into a shallow dish, and break it up into chunks.

Pour over:
½ cup olive oil
salt and pepper to taste
juice of 2 lemons

Serve as a salad with greens. It is also excellent with slices of ripe avocado and red onion.

CUCINALA COME VUOI, MA SEPRE COCUZZA É.

"Cook squash anyway you like, but it's always squash."
No matter how you slice it, it's always baloney.

Side Dishes

Frittedda (Vegetable Stew)

Potato Pancakes

Boiled Big Fava Beans

Stuffed Artichokes

Cousin Vito's Zucchini Patties

Frocia (Asparagus Omelet)

Frittata (Potato and Red Pepper Omelet)

Frittedda
(Vegetable Stew)

Frittedda is a stew of artichokes, fava beans, peas, and asparagus flavored with fennel. It is eaten in early spring when these vegetables first appear, and it represents a celebration of the earth's renewal. In the spring, we always had an abundance of fava beans at the Winery. My brother, Ross, grew at least an acre of them every year. Fortunately, friends and relatives enjoyed them as much as we did. We would often see grateful relatives eating the beans raw as they picked boxes of them to take home.

In a heavy pot over medium heat, heat:
>½ **cup extra virgin olive oil**

Add and sauté until translucent:
>**6 scallions, white and green parts, chopped**

Add:
>**8 oz. artichoke hearts (defrosted, if you are using frozen)**
>**1½ pounds fava beans, shelled**
>**1¼ pounds asparagus, cut into 1¼-inch pieces**
>**8 oz. sweet peas (defrosted, if you are using frozen)**
>**¼ pound fennel leaves and stems, cleaned and chopped fine**

Mix everything together and stir. Cover and cook on low heat (for about 30 minutes), stirring from time to time and adding a little water if necessary. There should be very little liquid remaining when it is ready to be served.

Serve this dish hot with:
>**a good bread**
>**a good Italian cheese, such as provolone, caciocavallo, or Parmesan**

Potato Pancakes

When I was growing up, we did not eat meat on Fridays. For Friday dinners we often had these potato pancakes as a side dish with fish.

In a large pot of boiling water, cook until tender:

8 potatoes, peeled and cut in half

Transfer the potatoes to a large bowl and mash well.

Add and mix gently:

4 eggs
1 cup bread crumbs
¼ cup Italian parsley, minced
½ cup grated Parmesan cheese
salt and pepper to taste

Shape mixture into ovals 2 inches wide and 3 inches long.

In a frying pan, heat:

½ cup olive oil

Add the pancakes and cook over medium high heat until golden brown (about 3 minutes on each side). Keep warm and serve.

Boiled Big
Fava Beans

During fava season, some of the pods grew larger than the others. We used these larger fava beans as appetizers or in side dishes.

In a pot large enough to accommodate the beans, boil:
> **water**
> **1 Tablespoon salt**

Drop in and boil (for 10 minutes):
> **large fava beans with their jackets (smooth outer covering)**

Drain, cool, and sprinkle with:
> **wine vinegar (such as Bernardo Winery wine vinegar)**
> **olive oil (such as Bernardo Winery olive oil)**
> **salt and pepper to taste**

Enjoy a glass of red wine while you pop these into your mouth and remove the "jackets."

Growing Fava Beans at The Bernardo Winery

MOGLI E BUIO DAI PAESI TUOI.
"Your wife and your oxen—buy them in your own town."
Buy locally!

Stuffed Artichokes

For this recipe, pick the freshest artichokes you can find. To determine the freshness, squeeze the "leaves." Fresh artichokes will squeak when squeezed.

Prepare:
> **4 large artichokes**

Cut off the stem, and peel off the tough outer bottom leaves. Use scissors to clip off the thorny tops of the leaves until you get almost to the top of the artichoke, and then cut off the entire rest of the top.

Rinse thoroughly while spreading the leaves apart. Place top side down in the sink to drain.

Prepare Stuffing:
In a large bowl, mix well:

> **1 cup fresh bread crumbs**   **⅓ cup olive oil**
> **1 cup Panko**   **3 Tablespoons parsley, chopped**
> **½ cup grated Parmesan cheese**   **3 cloves fresh garlic, pressed**

Stuff Prepared Artichokes:
Starting at the bottom, rotate artichokes while opening the leaves. Sprinkle the breadcrumbs into cavities. Continue to open and sprinkle until all of the leaves have been "stuffed." Make sure you get plenty of the crumbs into the flat top of the artichoke.

Bake Artichokes:
Place the artichokes in a deep pan, pour 2 cups of water into the bottom of the pan, and drizzle the tops of the artichokes with ¼ cup of olive oil.

Cover the pan *tightly* with foil. When you bake the artichokes, the effect should be that you are almost "steaming" them.

Bake at 350° (for 1 to 2 hours depending on the size of the artichokes). You will know that they are done when you can easily pull off the leaves.

They can be served hot or at room temperature.

Cousin Vito's
Zucchini Patties

Grapevines and Olive Branches

My cousin Vito was a lovable, fun, and all-around great guy who loved and was loved by everyone. He was the life of every gathering, and a good cook. His zucchini patties are one of my most requested recipes.

In a large bowl, mix together:
>**6 zucchini, unpeeled and grated**
>**3 potatoes, boiled and mashed**
>**1½ cups fresh bread crumbs**
>**½ cup grated Parmesan cheese**
>**¼ cup parsley, minced**
>**½ cup onion, finely minced**
>**2 cloves garlic, crushed**
>**4 eggs**
>**1 teaspoon salt**
>**freshly ground pepper to taste**

Form patties into 3-inch circles.

In a large frying pan, heat:
>**½ cup vegetable oil**

Fry the patties in batches (avoid crowding them) until golden brown. Remove to a paper towel to drain.

Serve them immediately or at room temperature.

Frocia
(Asparagus Omelet)

An easy baked omelet that can be an anytime snack or side dish. It all happens quickly, so before you begin, set your oven to broil.

Prepare:
Trim woody ends off and cut into 1-inch pieces:
> **1 pound asparagus**

In an oven-proof frying pan, heat:
> **2 Tablespoons extra virgin olive oil**

Add and sauté until tender (for about 10 minutes). Cover after 3 minutes, and do not allow to brown:
> **the prepared asparagus**
> **¼ teaspoon salt**
> **pepper to taste**

In a medium-sized bowl, beat together:
> **6 eggs**
> **½ cup grated Parmigiano-Reggiano cheese**

Pour the egg mixture over the cooked asparagus. Use a fork or knife to distribute the asparagus evenly in a single layer, and cook on high until the eggs are set.

Place the skillet with the eggs under the broiler (for 2 minutes). Watch for a golden crust to form.

(If you do not have an oven-proof skillet, wrap aluminum foil around the handle of your skillet, and proceed.)

Remove from the oven. Cut and serve.

Frittata
(Potato and Red Pepper Omelet)

Frittatas are relatively quick and versatile. They can be served warm, at room temperature, or cold. Make sure your pan is not too hot. Before you pour in the egg mixture, your pan should be warm enough to set the bottom of the frittata but not so hot that the bottom browns too quickly and becomes tough.

Set your oven to broil.

Peel and slice thin:
> **4 medium potatoes**

Chop into ½-inch pieces:
> **1 red bell pepper**

Slice very thinly:
> **1 onion**

In a medium bowl, mix and beat with a fork:
> **8 eggs**
> **1 teaspoon salt**
> **fresh ground pepper**
> **½ cup grated Parmesan cheese**

In a large frying pan over medium to medium-high heat, heat:
> **4 Tablespoons olive oil**

Add and cook covered (for 20 minutes or until the vegetables are soft):
> **the prepared potatoes, red pepper, and onion**

Pour the egg mixture over the cooked vegetables. Use a fork or knife to distribute the ingredients evenly, and continue to cook until the eggs are set (about 5 minutes).

Put the frying pan into the oven to broil (for 5 minutes). Make sure that it browns evenly.

Let the frittata rest for a few minutes, then slide onto a plate or tray. Cut and serve.

LA PENA MATURA CADE SOLA.

"A ripe fruit will fall by itself."
Everything in its own time.

Desserts

Baked Figs

Giuggiulena (Sesame Seed Cookies)

Aunt Josie's Anise Biscotti

Ricotta Cheesecake

Cubbaita (Almond and Sesame Seed Candy)

Persimmon Cookies

Aunt Jenny's Fig Cookies

Baked Figs

Grapevines and Olive Branches

All the ingredients for this dish grew on the Winery's property, and we had beehives that gave us wonderful honey. This is a delicious and healthy summer dessert.

Coat a shallow baking dish (like Pyrex) large enough to hold all the figs with:
1 Tablespoon butter

In the prepared dish place:
12-16 ripe figs (black or green)

Sprinkle with:
2 Tablespoons sugar

Bake at 400° (for 8-12 minutes). Remove from oven and allow to cool.

Toast the Walnuts:
Lower the oven temperature to 350°.

In a pie pan, place and toast (for 10 minutes):
½ cup walnuts, chopped

Prepare the Glaze:
In a heavy saucepan, bring to a boil and cook until thickened for (2-3 minutes):
¾ cup honey
juice of 1 lemon

Stir and cook until mixture is very thick. Add and stir to combine:
2 Tablespoons butter

Assemble the Dish:
Spoon the glaze over the figs, and garnish with the toasted walnuts. Serve at room temperature.

Giuggiulena
(Sesame Seed Cookies)

This is a wonderfully festive biscotti-style cookie—crunchy, sweet, and nutty, all at the same time.

With an electric mixer, beat until creamy:
> **2 sticks unsalted butter, room temperature**
> **1 cup sugar**

Beat in one at a time:
> **3 large eggs**

Add and beat:
> **1 teaspoon baking powder**
> **½ teaspoon salt**
> **1 teaspoon vanilla**

Stir in, ½ cup at a time:
> **4 cups flour**

Continue mixing until the mixture forms a smooth, pliable dough.

In a pie plate or shallow soup bowl, place:
> **1 cup milk**

In a second pie plate or shallow soup bowl, place:
> **2 cups sesame seeds**

To form each cookie, pinch off a small piece of dough and shape it into a log ½ inch in diameter and about 2½ inches long. Dip each log into the milk, and then roll in sesame seeds.

Place the logs on a cookie sheet lined with parchment paper.

Bake at 350° (for 15-20 minutes or until the logs are golden).

Transfer the cookies to racks to cool.

Aunt Josie's Anise Biscotti

My mother's aunt always made these cookies for us when she visited. Anise and almonds were grown at the Winery.

On a sheet pan, place:
> **2 cups almonds, chopped**

Toast the almonds in the oven (for 10 minutes).

In the bowl of a mixer, cream together:
> **2 cups shortening**
> **2 cups sugar**

Add and mix well:
> **5 cups flour**
> **handful of anise seeds (about ¼ cup)**
> **4 teaspoons baking powder**
> **7 eggs, beaten**

Add and blend well:
> **the toasted almonds**

Form the dough into 4 long logs, and slightly flatten to about 1 inch high.

Place the logs on a cookie sheet lined with parchment paper.

Bake at 350° (for 20-25 minutes). Let cool and cut logs into 1-inch slices. Place the slices on the cookie sheet, cut side down, and return to the oven to bake (for an additional 15 minutes).

Ricotta Cheesecake

Cheesecakes have been around since the fifteenth century, when early cookbooks described them as "cooked tart made from curd cheese, eggs, sugar, and spices." Ricotta Cheesecake, a traditional Italian recipe, is light and fluffy.

Separate:
> **8 eggs**

In a mixer, beat the egg whites until stiff, and remove them to a bowl.

Wipe out the mixer bowl, add and beat until whipped, and then remove to a bowl:
> **½ cup whipping cream**

Wipe out the mixer bowl, add and beat until smooth:
> **1 3-pound container of good quality ricotta**

Add and continue beating:
> **1½ cups sugar**
> **8 egg yolks**

Add and beat until incorporated:
> **½ cup flour**
> **grated rind of 1 lemon**

Fold egg whites and whipped cream into the ricotta mixture.

Turn mixture into a 12-inch springform pan which has been buttered and sprinkled with:
> **Graham cracker crumbs**

Bake at 425° (for 10 minutes). Lower the temperature to 350° and bake (for 1 hour longer). Turn off the heat, and allow the cheesecake to cool in the oven with the door closed.

Cubbaita
(Almond and Sesame Seed Candy)

The ancient, sweet Cubbaita is made throughout Italy, but it was originally developed by the Arabs who lived in Sicily. My great-aunt Josie, who made this candy for the holidays, shared this recipe with me.

In a heavy pan over medium heat, melt until liquid:
> **2 cups sugar**

Add and stir together quickly:
> **2 cups sesame seeds**
> **1½ cups whole almonds**
> **1 Tablespoon honey**

Pour the mixture onto a marble surface that has been lightly oiled or sprinkled with water. Spread the candy and use an oiled rolling pin to flatten it. When it is cool, cut or break it into bite-sized pieces.

IMPARA DALL'ESPERIENZA DEGLI ALTRI.

"Learn from the experience of others."

Persimmon Cookies

Persimmon trees are one of the first fruit trees cultivated by man, beginning in China over 2000 years ago. The persimmon arrived in Europe through France in the nineteenth century as an ornamental plant. Italy's first persimmon was planted in Florence's Boboli Gardens in 1871.

If your persimmons are not fully ripe, put them in a paper bag with an apple or a pear to ripen them more quickly.

In a small bowl, combine:
> **1 teaspoon baking soda**
> **1 cup persimmon pulp (the pulp of 2 persimmons)**

In a mixing bowl, combine and beat until creamy:
> **1 cup sugar**
> **½ cup shortening**

Add and mix together:
> **2 cups flour**
> **1 egg**
> **½ teaspoon salt**
> **½ teaspoon cinnamon**

Blend into the mixture:
> **persimmon mixture**

Add:
> **1 cup raisins**
> **1 cup walnuts**

Chill (for 30 minutes).

Drop cookie mixture by spoonfuls onto a parchment-lined cookie sheet. Bake at 350° (for 15-20 minutes).

Aunt Jenny's Fig Cookies

Aunt Jenny (my mother's youngest sister) was our family "character." She was funny, a great baker, and the family hypochondriac—whatever illness someone had, she had it worse! Periodically, Aunt Jenny came to the Winery and baked for us. Fortunately, I asked for some of her recipes. This is one that is very traditional in Sicilian households, especially at Christmas.

Filling:
Combine the following and grind in a manual or electric grinder:

4 cups dried figs (stems snipped off)
2 cups raisins
1 large Hershey bar, broken into pieces
2 orange rinds, cut into pieces
juice of 2 oranges
1 cup citron (candied fruit)
2 Tablespoons honey

Dough:
In a bowl, combine and knead the ingredients together until pliable:

2 sticks butter, softened
1 cup sugar
6 eggs (save 2 whites)
enough flour to make a soft dough (about 4½ cups)

Refrigerate dough (for 30 minutes).

Remove dough from the refrigerator and turn onto a floured board. Cut a slice of the dough and roll into a 4x8-inch slab with a rolling pin. The dough should be about ¼ inch thick.

Spread the fig mixture along the length of the dough. Fold the dough over the mixture and press to seal. Roll the log into a circle, and then press to flatten. Cut the flattened log into 2-inch pieces. Place on a parchment-lined cookie sheet, and bake at 350° (for 15-18 minutes or until slightly browned). Cool on a rack.

Icing:
In a bowl, combine and mix until the consistency of thick cream:

2 cups powdered sugar
milk

Frost each cookie with a brush, and sprinkle with colored sprinkles.

PIZZICHI E BACI NON FANNO BUCHI.
"Kisses and pinches leave no scars."

Figs: One of Man's Original Food

Figs enjoy a rich history. They are one of the first fruits cultivated by humans. Discovered in the town of Jericho, in the Jordan Valley, they date back to 9400–9200 BC, long before the use and cultivation of many common grains and beans.

SOME FIG VARIETIES INCLUDE:

Celeste: A purplish-brown fig. When ripe, it's quite sweet and moist.

Calimyrna: Has a nut-like flavor and delightful golden skin.

Dottato: A common fig in the Italian area of Calabria. It has a green skin with a whitish/golden flesh that tastes creamy, sweet, and light. It dries well.

Kadota: An American version of the Italian "Dottato" fig. Since it has fewer seeds, it is often canned or dried..

Mission: Was named "Mission" to honor the original mission fathers who planted fig trees all along the California coast.

Index

A

Almonds
    Aunt Josie's Anise Biscotti, 166
    Cubbaita (Almond and Sesame
      Seed Candy), 170
Amogue (Steak Sauce), 120
Anaheim Peppers, Roasted, 34
Anchovies
    Pane Consado (Fixed Bread), 102
    Red Pepper Bruschetta, 26
    Sicilian Summer Salad, 52
    Spaghetti Puttanesca, 92
Anise Biscotti, Aunt Josie's, 166
Appetizers
    Arancini (Stuffed Fried Rice Balls), 38
    Caponata (Vegetable Relish), 24
    Carduni Fritti (Fried Cardoons), 44
    Fried Pumpkin with Mint, 42
    Goat Cheese, Fig and Walnut
      Bruschetta, 28
    Green Olives with Orange and Fennel
      Seed, 30
    Red Pepper Bruschetta, 26
    Roasted Anaheim Peppers, 34
    Stuffed Mushrooms, 46

    Stuffed Red Peppers, 32
    Zucchini con Pancetta (Zucchini
      Bacon Spread), 36
Arancini (Stuffed Fried Rice Balls), 38
Artichokes
    Carduni Fritti (Fried Cardoons), 44
    Frittedda (Vegetable Stew), 146
    Stuffed Artichokes, 152
Asparagus
    Frittedda (Vegetable Stew), 146
    Frocia (Asparagus Omelet), 156
Aunt Jenny's Fig Cookies, 174
Aunt Josie's Anise Biscotti, 166

B

Bacon Spread, Zucchini with, 36
Baked Figs, 162
Baked Ziti, 84
Beans
    Fava. *See* Fava beans
    Palermo-Style Salad, 50
    Penne with Escarole and Beans, 76
    Sicilian Summer Salad, 52
Beef
    Arancini (Stuffed Fried Rice Balls), 38

Braciola, 122
Meatballs, 124
Spedini, 108
Sunday Tomato Sauce with Meats, 126
Biscotti, Aunt Josie's Anise, 166
Blood Orange and Fennel Salad, 54
Boiled Big Fava Beans, 150
Braciola
Braciola, 122
Sunday Tomato Sauce with Meats, 126
Braided Rolls, My Mothers, 98
Bread
My Mother's Braided Rolls, 98
Pane Consado (Fixed Bread), 102
Panelli, 100
Bread crumbs. *See* Stuffed Red Peppers
Broccoli
Rigatoni with Broccoli, 70
Sautéed Broccoli Rabe with Sausage, 114
Bruschetta
Goat Cheese, Fig and Walnut Bruschetta, 28
Red Pepper Bruschetta, 26

C
Calamari, Insalata di Mare (Seafood Salad), 138
Caponata (Vegetable Relish), 24
Carduni Fritti (Fried Cardoons), 44
Cauliflower, Orecchiette with, 72
Cheesecake, Ricotta, 168
Chicken
Chicken Cacciatore, 116
Chicken Cutlets, 112
Cookies
Aunt Jenny's Fig Cookies, 174
Aunt Josie's Anise Biscotti, 166
Giuggiulena (Sesame Seed Cookies), 164

Persimmon Cookies, 172
Cousin Vito's Zucchini Patties, 154
Cubbaita (Almond and Sesame Seed Candy), 170
Cucuzza Longa, Homemade Pasta or Spaghetti with, 78

D
Dad's Salad Dressing, 58
Desserts and Sweets
Aunt Jenny's Fig Cookies, 174
Aunt Josie's Anise Biscotti, 166
Baked Figs, 162
Cubbaita (Almond and Sesame Seed Candy), 170
Giuggiulena (Sesame Seed Cookies), 164
Persimmon Cookies, 172
Ricotta Cheesecake, 168

E
Eggplant
Caponata (Vegetable Relish), 24
Zita with Eggplant, 80
Eggs
Frittedda (Vegetable Stew), 146
Frocia (Asparagus Omelet), 156
Escarole and Beans, Penne with, 76

F
Fava Beans
Boiled Big Fava Beans, 150
Frittedda (Vegetable Stew), 146
Homemade Pasta with Fava Beans, 66
Ross's Lamb and Fava Bean Stew, 106
Fennel
Blood Orange and Fennel Salad, 54
Frittedda (Vegetable Stew), 146
Green Olives with Orange and Fennel Seed, 30

Homemade Pasta with Fava Beans, 66
Linguini Finocchio con Sarde (Linguini
    with Fennel and Sardines), 94
Figs
    Aunt Jenny's Fig Cookies, 174
    Baked Figs, 162
    Goat Cheese, Fig and Walnut
        Bruschetta, 28
Fish and Seafood
    Insalata di Mare (Seafood Salad), 138
    Linguini Finocchio con Sarde (Linguini
        with Fennel and Sardines), 94
    Pane Consado (Fixed Bread), 102
    Red Pepper Bruschetta, 26
    Rollatine di Pesce Spada (Grilled
        Swordfish Rolls), 132
    Sicilian Summer Salad, 52
    Spaghetti Puttanesca, 92
    Swordfish Rolls in Tomato Sauce, 134
    Tuna Salad with Oil and Lemon, 142
Fixed Bread (Pane Consado), 102
Flavored bread crumbs. *See* Stuffed Red
        Peppers
Fried Cardoons (Carduni Fritti), 44
Fried Pumpkin with Mint, 42
Fried Rice Balls, Stuffed (Arancini), 38
Frittata (Potato and Red Pepper Omelet),
    158
Frittedda (Vegetable Stew), 146
Frocia (Asparagus Omelet), 156

G
Garlic
    Amogue (Steak Sauce), 120
    Linguini with Garlic and Oil, 86
    Roasted Leg of Lamb, 118
Giuggiulena (Sesame Seed Cookies), 164
Goat Cheese, Fig and Walnut Bruschetta,
    28
Green beans

Palermo-Style Salad, 50
Sicilian Summer Salad, 52
Green olives
    Caponata (Vegetable Relish), 24
    Green Olives with Orange and Fennel
        Seed, 30
    Insalata di Mare (Seafood Salad), 138
    Sicilian Summer Salad, 52
Green Olives with Orange and Fennel Seed,
    30
Grilled Swordfish Rolls (Rollatine di Pesce
    Spada), 132

H
Homemade Pasta, 64
Homemade Pasta or Spaghetti with Cucuzza
    Longa (Sicilian Squash), 78
Homemade Pasta with Fava Beans, 66

I
Insalata di Mare (Seafood Salad), 138

L
Lamb
    Roasted Leg of Lamb, 118
    Ross's Lamb and Fava Bean Stew, 106
Linguini
    Linguini Finocchio con Sarde (Linguini
        with Fennel and Sardines), 94
    Linguini with Garlic and Oil, 86
    Linguini with Marinara Sauce, 82

M
Marinara Sauce, Linguini with, 82
Meat and Poultry
    Amogue (Steak Sauce), 120
    Arancini (Stuffed Fried Rice Balls), 38
    Braciola, 122
    Chicken Cacciatore, 116
    Chicken Cutlets, 112

Meatballs, 124
Roasted Leg of Lamb, 118
Ross's Lamb and Fava Bean Stew, 106
Sausage with Peppers and Onions, 110
Sautéed Broccoli Rabe with Sausage,
    114
Spedini, 108
Sunday Tomato Sauce with Meats, 126
Meatballs
    Meatballs, 124
    Sunday Tomato Sauce with Meats, 126
Mint, Fried Pumpkin, with, 42
Mushrooms
    Chicken Cacciatore, 116
    Stuffed Mushrooms, 46
Mussels, Insalata di Mare (Seafood Salad),
    138
My Mother's Braided Rolls, 98

O
Olives
    Caponata (Vegetable Relish), 24
    Green Olives with Orange and Fennel
        Seed, 30
    Insalata di Mare (Seafood Salad), 138
    Red Pepper Bruschetta, 26
    Sautéed Broccoli Rabe with Sausage,
        114
    Sicilian Summer Salad, 52
    Spaghetti Puttanesca, 92
Omelets
    Frittata (Potato and Red Pepper
        Omelet), 158
    Frocia (Asparagus Omelet), 156
Onions
    Roasted Leg of Lamb, 118
    Sausage with Peppers and Onions, 110
Oranges
    Blood Orange and Fennel Salad, 54
    Green Olives with Orange and Fennel

Seed, 30
Orecchiette with Cauliflower, 72
Oregano Salad, Plum Tomato and, 56

P
Palermo-Style Salad, 50
Pane Consado (Fixed Bread), 102
Panelli, 100
Pasta
    Baked Ziti, 84
    Homemade Pasta, 64
    Homemade Pasta or Spaghetti with
        Cucuzza Longa (Sicilian Squash), 78
    Homemade Pasta with Fava Beans, 66
    Linguini Finocchio con Sarde (Linguini
        with Fennel and Sardines), 94
    Linguini with Garlic and Oil, 86
    Linguini with Marinara Sauce, 82
    Orecchiette with Cauliflower, 72
    Penne with Escarole and Beans, 76
    Penne with Pesto Sauce, 90
    Penne with Vodka Sauce, 88
    Rigatoni with Broccoli, 70
    Spaghetti Puttanesca, 92
    Zita with Eggplant, 80
Penne
    Penne with Escarole and Beans, 76
    Penne with Pesto Sauce, 90
    Penne with Vodka Sauce, 88
Peppers
    Roasted Anaheim Peppers, 34
    Sausage with Peppers and Onions, 110
    Also see Red peppers
Persimmon Cookies, 172
Pesto Sauce, Penne with, 90
Pine nuts (pignoli)
    Braciola, 122
    Caponata (Vegetable Relish), 24
    Linguini Finocchio con Sarde (Linguini
        with Fennel and Sardines), 94

Penne with Pesto Sauce, 90
Rollatine di Pesce Spada (Grilled Swordfish Rolls), 132
Stuffed Red Peppers, 32
Plum Tomato and Oregano Salad, 56
Pork
Meatballs, 124
Sunday Tomato Sauce with Meats, 126
Potatoes
Cousin Vito's Zucchini Patties, 154
Frittata (Potato and Red Pepper Omelet), 158
Palermo-Style Salad, 50
Potato Pancakes, 148
Roasted Leg of Lamb, 118
Prepared flavored bread crumbs. *See* Stuffed Red Peppers
Pumpkin, Fried with Mint, 42

R
Raisins
Aunt Jenny's Fig Cookies, 174
Linguini Finocchio con Sarde (Linguini with Fennel and Sardines), 94
Persimmon Cookies, 172
Rollatine di Pesce Spada (Grilled Swordfish Rolls), 132
Red Pepper Bruschetta, 26
Red peppers
Frittata (Potato and Red Pepper Omelet), 158
Red Pepper Bruschetta, 26
Stuffed Red Peppers, 32
Relish, Vegetable (Caponata) , 24
Rice Balls, Stuffed Fried (Arancini), 38
Ricotta Cheesecake, 168
Rigatoni with Broccoli, 70
Roasted Anaheim Peppers, 34
Roasted Leg of Lamb, 118
Rollatine di Pesce Spada (Grilled Swordfish Rolls), 132
Rolls
My Mother's Braided Rolls, 98
Pane Consado (Fixed Bread), 102
Panelli, 100
Rosemary
Amogue (Steak Sauce), 120
Roasted Leg of Lamb, 118
Ross's Lamb and Fava Bean Stew, 106

S
Salad dressing
Dad's Salad Dressing, 58
Vince's Salad, 60
Salads
Blood Orange and Fennel Salad, 54
Dad's Salad Dressing, 58
Palermo-Style Salad, 50
Plum Tomato and Oregano Salad, 56
Seafood Salad, 138
Sicilian Summer Salad, 52
Tuna Salad with Oil and Lemon, 142
Vince's Salad, 60
Sardines, Linguini with Fennel and (Linguini Finocchio con Sarde), 94
Sausage
Sausage with Peppers and Onions, 110
Sautéed Broccoli Rabe with Sausage, 114
Sunday Tomato Sauce with Meats, 126
Seafood Salad (Insalata di Mare), 138
Sesame Seeds
Cubbaita (Almond and Sesame Seed Candy), 170
Giuggiulena (Sesame Seed Cookies), 164
Shrimp, Insalata di Mare (Seafood Salad), 138
Sicilian Summer Salad, 52
Side Dishes

Boiled Big Fava Beans, 150
Cousin Vito's Zucchini Patties, 154
Frittata (Potato and Red Pepper
    Omelet), 158
Frittedda (Vegetable Stew), 146
Frocia (Asparagus Omelet), 156
Potato Pancakes, 148
Stuffed Artichokes, 152
Spaghetti
    Homemade Pasta or Spaghetti with
        Cucuzza Longa (Sicilian Squash), 78
    Homemade Pasta with Fava Beans, 66
    Linguini with Garlic and Oil, 86
    Linguini with Marinara Sauce, 82
    Spaghetti Puttanesca, 92
Spedini 108
Squash, Homemade Pasta or Spaghetti
    with Cucuzza Longa (Sicilian
        Squash), 78
Steak
    Braciola, 122
    Spedini, 108
Steak Sauce (Amogu), 120
Stew
    Frittedda (Vegetable Stew), 146
    Ross's Lamb and Fava Bean Stew, 106
Stuffed Artichokes, 152
Stuffed Fried Rice Balls (Arancini), 38
Stuffed Mushrooms, 46
Stuffed Red Peppers, 32
Summer Salad, Sicilian, 52
Sunday Tomato Sauce with Meats, 126
Swordfish
    Rollatine di Pesce Spada (Grilled
        Swordfish Rolls), 132

Swordfish Rolls in Tomato Sauce, 134

T
Tomatoes
    Amogue (Steak Sauce), 120
    Palermo-Style Salad, 50
    Plum Tomato and Oregano Salad, 56
    Sicilian Summer Salad, 52
    Sunday Tomato Sauce with Meats, 126
    Swordfish Rolls in Tomato Sauce, 134
Tuna Salad with Oil and Lemon, 142

V
Veal, Meatballs, 124
Vegetable Relish, (Caponata), 24
Vegetable Stew (Frittedda), 146
Vince's Salad, 60
Vodka Sauce, Penne with, 88

W
Walnuts
    Baked Figs, 162
    Goat Cheese, Fig and Walnut
        Bruschetta, 28
    Persimmon Cookies, 172

Z
Ziti
    Baked Ziti, 84
    Zita with Eggplant, 80
Zucchini
    Cousin Vito's Zucchini Patties, 154
    Zucchini con Pancetta (Zucchini Bacon
        Spread), 36

About the Authors

Nina Rizzo Renda (right)

Nina enjoyed a magical childhood at the historic Bernardo Winery, which has been in her family's talented hands for over a hundred years. Thanks to the Winery's lush and fertile offerings, Nina and her loved ones have always enjoyed fresh, seasonal ingredients in their home-cooked Sicilian food. Following in her father's footsteps, Nina became the cook of the extended family. She has built on the memories of her warm, loving, and hospitable childhood by sharing her family's history, philosophy, and recipes with you. Nourishing her relatives and guests with the Winery's crisp, flavorful fruits and vegetables has always brought Nina much joy. With this book, she invites you to share her family's Sicilian cuisine and to bring the love and warmth they have always shared to your family table.

Leslie May Rodwick (left)

Leslie grew up in Buenos Aires, Argentina, home to a huge Italian immigrant community. She continues to enjoy wonderful memories of the delicious Italian food she delighted in for so many years. Leslie has traveled extensively throughout Italy and was privileged to attend Marcella Hazan's Master Class in Italian Cooking in Venice, 1998. Her love of cooking has inspired her to attend additional cooking classes and develop her unique approach to formatting easy-to-follow recipes that incorporate ingredient lists within a recipe's instructions. Leslie's cookbook design is distinctive, and she hopes you enjoy not only her approach to cooking but also the flavors and aromas of the Bernardo Winery.